DISTRICT DUTIES

DURING THE REVOLT

DISTRICT DUTIES

DURING THE REVOLT

IN THE

NORTH-WEST PROVINCES OF INDIA,
IN 1857:

WITH

REMARKS ON SUBSEQUENT INVESTIGATIONS
DURING 1858-59.

BY

H. DUNDAS ROBERTSON,

BENGAL CIVIL SERVICE.

GYAN

Published by

Gyan Publishing House
5, Ansari Road
Daryaganj, New Delhi-110002
Phone: 011-47034999, 9811692060
E-mail: books@gyanbooks.com

Distribution Network
gyanbooks.com
India, USA, Canada, UK, Australia

ISBN: 978-81-212-7055-7 (PB)
First Published, 1859

2nd Impression 2024

Printed at: Gyan Press, Delhi.

DISTRICT DUTIES DURING THE REVOLT
Author: H. DUNDAS ROBERTSON

DISTRICT DUTIES

DURING THE REVOLT.

DISTRICT DUTIES

DURING THE REVOLT

IN THE

NORTH-WEST PROVINCES OF INDIA,

IN 1857:

WITH

REMARKS ON SUBSEQUENT INVESTIGATIONS

DURING 1858-59.

BY

H. DUNDAS ROBERTSON,

BENGAL CIVIL SERVICE.

LONDON:

SMITH, ELDER AND CO., 65, CORNHILL.

M.DCCC.LIX.

INTRODUCTION.

To account for the appearance of the following pages, it may be sufficient to state that I was detained some weeks in the capital of British India, by the impossibility of procuring a passage to England, in consequence of the large number of officers who were set at liberty by the close of hostilities, and who were eager to revisit their native country. I was tempted to employ the leisure thus unexpectedly placed at my command in recalling the scenes through which I passed; and this memorial of them, with the observations they suggested at the time, is now submitted to the serious consideration of the few for whom India possesses more than that ephemeral interest excited during the progress of the revolt in 1857.

The first, and in fact the major, portion of this

book will furnish a record of events in a district under the government of the North-West Provinces, where, notwithstanding mutiny and rebellion, British authority was successfully maintained by some half-dozen Englishmen, left to their own resources, without the hope even of assistance from European troops.

Though at times associated with others, my position frequently became that of the only European actor in the scenes described, which, combined with the character of many of the incidents, has necessitated the form of a personal narrative when referring to this district; but, my object being the elucidation of a subject of general interest, all merely personal adventures, not illustrating any characteristic features of those stormy times or of native character, have been omitted.

It was my intention to treat the subject of the last few chapters at considerable length, but managing to escape from Calcutta a fortnight earlier than I at first expected, this portion of the book remained in outline as first sketched. On arriving in England my original design might have been completed, but finding such a thorough distaste in this country for everything connected with India, I deemed it rather fortunate than otherwise that I had not devoted more time to that part of my subject. The book as it is may, however, help towards the understanding of a difficult subject, yet one of great importance both to the interests of England and India.

No excuse is offered for bringing forward some defects in the old native army in Bengal. I was long engaged in the investigation of the cases of mutineer sepoys, and a few of the errors that became apparent in the course of these investigations are referred to, with the hope that the remarks may be useful in guarding our Indian empire against total wreck on the very rocks on which it has once already grounded.

As a reference to the subject of my position during the revolt might be considered necessary, it may be here stated that, at the commencement of the outbreak in May, 1857, I was, as it is termed in the North-West Provinces, a joint magistrate in the Saharunpore district. In September of that year

I also became officiating collector of that district; and towards the close of 1857, in conjunction with Messrs. J. C. Wilson and T. D. Forsyth, I was placed on a commission for the investigation and trial of cases connected with the mutiny and rebellion, being vested with jurisdiction extending over the North-West Provinces, Oude, Bengal Proper, and Central India. In this commission I remained till its proceedings were closed.

London, August 2nd, 1859.

CONTENTS.

DISTRICT DUTIES DURING THE REVOLT.

CHAPTER I.

Situation and resources of the Saharunpore district—Origin of its mixed population and numerous forts—Notes on the inhabitants generally of the North-West Provinces and of Oude—Contrast between the natural features of this district and the rest of the North-West—Advantages, or otherwise, of its canal system—Importance of certain restrictions in the distribution of the water required for purposes of irrigation—Class of cultivators in this district—City, European station, and fort of Saharunpore—Our strength at the commencement of the outbreak in May, 1857—Political and financial importance of Saharunpore during the revolt.

THE Saharunpore district, to which the following remarks chiefly refer, is situated in the north-western corner of the North-West Provinces of Hindustan; its eastern boundary being formed by the Ganges, and its western by the Jumna, both traced from the point where they issue from the Himalaya Mountains. Though only distant from Meeruth between seventy and eighty miles, and but little farther from Delhi, the position of Saharunpore is rather isolated, and this isolation became during the revolt of 1857 an important feature of strength as long as internal mutiny and insurrection could be repressed. The Mozuffurnugur district, stretching along our southern boundary, did indeed rise from an early date in open revolt, but it was externally our only weak point.

Not only did two large rivers, the Ganges and Jumna, very materially protect the eastern and western boundaries of this district, but a range of uninhabitable mountains screened us with their friendly shelter from the north, and would have been of great importance had the hill tribes risen in revolt. The Sewalik range, from their southern watershed, bound the Saharunpore district to the north-east, extending from Hurdwar, the point at which the Ganges emerges from the Himalayas, to Kharah, where the Jumna makes its first appearance. These hills are a rugged, precipitous, sub-Himalayan range, with an elevation averaging some 3,000 feet above the level of the sea. They here consist almost entirely of a loose boulder formation, covered with brushwood, though in the gorges and lower hills, where the soil is deeper, fine forest trees are met with, surrounded by a dense grass and bamboo jungle. Throughout the whole range, little or no water is to be found during the hot season, so that these hills can never be of much value even as pasture-lands. Between this portion of the Sewaliks and the great Himalayan range is situated the valley of the Deyrah Dhoon, one day destined to become a vast tea plantation; and to the north of the Dhoon are the Himalayan sanitaria of Mussouree and Landour, some seventy miles distant from the town of Saharunpore. The length of the Saharunpore district is nearly seventy miles, its breadth some sixty, with a population of more than three-quarters of a million.*

With the exception of the Khaatah Rajpoots inhabiting the most healthy portion in the south of the district, and the roving Bunjarahs in the north, this population becomes, from the month of August to the end of the year, the most fever-stricken race that I have seen in any district in the North-West. They are, moreover, a most mongrel mixture of Moghuls, Puthans, Brahmuns, Goojurs, Rajpoots, Ranghurs, Ghâras, with an endless collection of nondescripts, generally the worst of their kind. The human species is said to be improved by intermixture, but in India persons of different races and creeds never intermarry. Though located together for several hundred years, and constituting apparently one community, they generally continue as distinct as if they had all inhabited different countries, pertinaciously retaining the national peculiarities and the characteristic virtues and vices of their ancestors. The extraordinary mingling of races in the popu-

* Eight hundred and fifty thousand at the last census, though now probably fully a million.

lation, notwithstanding their distinctness, has arisen from the circumstance that Saharunpore had long the misfortune of being a frontier district, laid claim to and overrun in turns by Afghans, Goorkhas, and Seikhs. To assist in holding so troublesome a province, its lands were constantly parcelled out by the Mahomedan emperors of Delhi to any adventurers who would engage to construct a fort,* and bring a certain number of human beings as settlers in their train, no matter of what stamp or race they were composed. The turbulent offscourings of Hindustan were consequently here collected, and, even up to the present day, never seem to have thriven in a portion of the country which is justly termed the garden of the North-West.

The general temperature of this district is much cooler than other portions of the North-West Provinces, the natural result of its high latitude, 30° north, and of its elevation, which varies in different localities from a thousand to twelve hundred feet above the level of the sea. Nevertheless, to those whom fever and ague have made their victims, the extensive Khâdir lands and swampy jungles of the district is hardly favourable. The snowy ranges of the Himalayas tower over the district, and the whole

* The banks of the Jumna throughout the Saharunpore district bear testimony to the serious difficulty that existed in holding this tract, as they are covered with the ruins of old forts, some of which are of Marhattah, and others of Hindustani construction.

of its northern half exhibits an undulating surface, well watered by numerous streams percolating through and appearing below the Sewaliks, which, combined with the custom of hedging the fields, gives this portion of the district at certain seasons of the year a peculiarly English appearance. It is, in fact, the only district in the North-West Provinces,*

* The inhabitants of the North-West Provinces and Oude are, both amongst themselves and by the residents of other portions of India, termed Hindustanis, in distinction to Bengalese, Marhattahs, Madrasees, and the various races which inhabit the peninsula. The North-West Provinces and Oude are, by the natives, looked upon as Hindustan Proper. Now that Oude belongs to the British Government, the designation "North-West Provinces and Oude" might cease to describe this tract when a more appropriate term exists among the residents of the country conveying the correct impression that this is the fountain-head of the lingua Franca, or Hindustani, of India, as also the seat of its most venerated religious and historical associations. Oude and the North-West Provinces, where the races are identical, being united under one government, as was, with the exception of the Delhi territory, formerly the arrangement under the old Mahomedan viceroyalty of Oude, the Saugor, Nurbudda, and other tracts in Central India, now governed from the North-West, being added to Nagpore, &c., at present under the Supreme Government in Calcutta, might be placed under a distinct government of their own. The present confused jumble would thus be formed into two separate governments of Hindustan Proper and Central India, while the welfare of our extensive and important Central Indian possessions would be better secured than is at present possible, in consequence of their distance from Calcutta and the North-West. Such a division, moreover, would obviate misconceptions amongst those whose tenure of office generally expires just as a slight knowledge of the political divisions of the country has been acquired. In using the term Hindustani in this book, the residents of the North-West Provinces and Oude are alone referred to.

with the exception of two or three bordering on the Terai, or strip of jungle running along the foot of the Himalayas, where the eye is not wearied by that boundless expanse of interminable plains cut up by sluggish, muddy streams, relieved alone by the square, sombre mangoe groves, in which every tree seems to have been produced, if not exactly at the same birth, at any rate of the same parentage with every other tree in every other grove. All the trees in each grove having been planted together, their size, height, branches, leaves, bark—I should not wonder, the very insects, certainly the pigs and children—are the same; one grove differs from another in nought but age, and age succeeds to changeless age. They and the whole aspect of a country rich both in the fertility of its soil and the natural talent of its races, are a fitting illustration of that deep, dead level produced by the unvarying, unprogressive caste prejudices which, as with an adamantine chain, fetter an entire race, body and soul.

Independently of its beauty, and at times the magnificence of its scenery, the Saharunpore district possesses many important natural, and also artificial advantages. The facilities for irrigation from the Ganges Canal on the east, with the Eastern Jumna Canal on the west, should, when combined with a favourable climate and rich soil, render this at no very distant date one of the most productive and valuable tracts in the North-West. These canals do not, however, at present confer benefits on the surrounding lands unaccompanied by serious disadvantages when the water is carelessly distributed; and, if the supply of water be not regulated according to its effects on the various soils, the irrigated lands may yet become a barren waste, and produce only a pauper population. A considerable extent of land, watered by the Western Jumna Canal, has already, as is well known in India, been seriously deteriorated by the action of the water; and I have seen some soils injuriously affected by the irrigation from the Eastern Jumna Canal. The Ganges Canal being a late construction, the effect of its waters on particular soils is not yet apparent.

The natives, fully alive to the dangerous results of irrigation from the Jumna canals, are totally ignorant of the causes producing this deterioration of the soil. They observe that the water supplied by the Jumna canals putrefies, as they suppose, on certain lands, when they are flooded for irrigational purposes, some two or three days sooner than on other lands; and this, doubtless, indicates the chemical action at work on that particular soil. The Himalayan chain abounding in granite, gneiss, limestone, and other rocks producing the inorganic elements, the rivers passing through these mountains are affected accordingly; and the Jumna, when it issues from the mountains, though a beautifully clear stream, evidently carries with it a large quantity of the inorganic substances and salts in solution, which, though increasing the fertility of the soil, where organic acids predominate, really deteriorates for the time those in which there is a deficiency of vegetable mould or organic acids, by imparting a superabundance of the inorganic. There is no reason, however, why this deterioration should be permanent in its results, if proper measures be adopted to remedy the evil. By prohibiting the supply of canal water during the dry season to the injured districts, the rain-water, which is largely impregnated with vegetable and animal matter, would probably in a few years alter the proportions of the organic and inorganic acids, while an improvement might be still more rapidly effected by inducing the cultivators to make a more liberal use of manure.

But I may here call attention to the fact that compensating elements are not wanting even in the resources of the canal system itself. It has often struck me that the water possesses at certain seasons all the elements necessary for restoring soil thus injured to its full vigour. It is during the dry season alone that these canal waters are impregnated with a superabundance of inorganic substances. During the rainy season, and particularly when the south-west monsoon first sets in, all the Himalayan rivers carry down with them a vast quantity of decayed animal and vegetable matter, which in the course of years has formed those rich deposits, called Khâdir lands, near their banks, and which are yearly increasing, enriched by the periodical inundations. Could not the canals, then, be so regulated as to supply from time to time this rich alluvium to the lands which have been injured by the water distributed during the dry season? To effect this, it only requires that the water from the Ganges and Jumna be freely admitted into these canals during the rainy season, when the rivers are flooded, and, though alterations might to a certain extent be necessary in the regulating agencies now employed at the source of the canals, the results would soon repay the expense that would be incurred.

Irrigation from the Ganges Canal has not been carried on for a sufficiently long period to test the effects of the water on the lands subjected to its influence; nor has it yet been generally adopted by the natives within a reasonable distance of its source. I say within a reasonable distance, because in the Ganges Canal the water may change its character, and all its originally injurious elements may be neutralized after it has been conveyed a hundred miles, or even less, from its source. The water, after travelling a considerable distance from the hills, may in its course have become impregnated with other salts, percolating through the bed of the canal, which may counteract the effects of those inorganic elements derived from the detritus of the various rocks in the Himalayas forming the bed of the Ganges, which, judging from the course of that river, must be very similar to those affecting the water of the Jumna; so that, after all, caution here also will be requisite.

As irrigation from the various canals in the North-West Provinces is yearly increasing, it has become important to the interests both of the people and the Government that the action of the water on the various soils should be fully understood, the results annually examined, and irrigation checked where injury is apparent; or we may some day awake to discover that half the country, like the banks of the Western Jumna Canal at the present time, has been converted into a desert. From the extent of land in the Saharunpore district capable of being brought under canal irrigation, an enlightened control exercised in the distribution of the water may yet form one of the most important steps towards its ultimate prosperity. With its extensive canal system thus rendered permanently beneficial, the Saharunpore district at once becomes extremely valuable, for its rich lands are capable of supporting an enormous population, and yielding a large revenue to the State.

All that Saharunpore now requires is population, with the increase of which the cultivated area will be enlarged and the climate rapidly improved, though jungle land in India when first ploughed up is extremely unhealthy, and the early progress consequently slow. The promoters of Christianity might with advantage plant Christian villages on these waste lands. In the more thickly peopled tracts it is by no means easy to purchase out the occupants, or procure land. There, moreover, the prejudices of the people are more deeply rooted than generally amongst this mongrel race. Any person wandering through this district would be at once struck by the paucity of Temples or Musjids,* particularly if he had lately come from the Benares or Cawnpore direction. Of the best class of cultivators, Jâts, Khachees, Khoormees, &c., there are few, though a clan called Ghâras are industrious and tolerably numerous, being the only race of good Mahomedan cultivators I have met with in the North-West; still the capabilities of the district are but poorly developed, and the cultivation generally is of the rudest and most improvident description.

The town of Saharunpore is situated on the right bank of a small clear stream rising in a swamp about seven miles north of the city, which eventually unites with the river Dumola some fifteen miles to the south-east of the town. Its population is estimated at from 35,000 to 40,000 souls, a large proportion of the residents being Mahomedans. In former times this town possessed a bad reputation for its turbulence. The station of Saharunpore, by which is meant the

* Temple, or Shewalla,—a Hindoo place of worship in distinction to Musjid, the Mahomedan.

various civil offices or other government buildings, with the residences of the government servants, is distant from the city some two miles.

The Europeans reside chiefly on the left bank of the stream above referred to, and the houses are generally surrounded by rich gardens and extensive grounds, while the fine botanical gardens between the city and a portion of the civil lines make an agreeable retreat during the hot season, the coolness of their shady drives and walks being fully appreciated even by the denizens of the forest, for I have known three leopards killed here in one morning. A small church embedded in a selection of some of the finest Indian forest trees forms a pleasing object in the centre of the station, while the American Mission has built a second nearer to the city. On the northern confines of the station is a compact little fort, built by a General Macleod when this place was a British frontier station, but on this ceasing to be the case, so utterly had all thoughts for the future been disregarded, that of all things in the world the civil gaol had been here formed, and monopolized almost the entire space within its ramparts. When the revolt commenced, we possessed no other building to which the prisoners could with security have been removed, so as to enable us to prepare this place for defence, had it been our intention to hold the fort if driven from the station. But yet a more serious objection existed to holding this rather strong little place.

At Saharunpore extensive stables for the stud-horses were necessary, and not only had some of these been built within musket range of the walls of the fort, but the ditches and mud-walls of the paddocks were run up so close to the place that from this cover every man defending it could have been picked off. Saharunpore has the unfortunate reputation of being considered unhealthy, but this fort, curiously enough, has been found the reverse, as the civil prisoners confined within its walls continue healthy when cholera and other diseases are prevalent in the neighbourhood. This fort being a modern construction, strong for its class, and commanding a portion of the country rather important to our communications with the Punjaub, it might not be too great a stretch of foresight here to station a company of European Artillery with their guns; the native prisoners might at the same time be transferred elsewhere, and those portions of the stud stables, or embankments, within range of the fort-walls demolished.

Saharunpore before the outbreak was essentially a civil station. Beyond the ordinary civil staff of a district in the North-West Provinces, there were three military officers, a gentleman in charge of the stud, two engineer officers attached to the Eastern Jumna Canal, and a doctor in charge of the botanical gardens, besides some missionaries. Some of these were absent on leave, and others of them left the station when the disturbances broke out, so that the Europeans present at the most critical time, including the clerks, numbered only six or seven persons; the Eurasians, who could hardly be regarded as a resource in the last extremity, being numerically but a little stronger. The guard over the civil treasury consisted of a party of sepoys some seventy or eighty strong, under their native commanding officer, a soobahdar; and these were relieved every three months from Moradabad by similar detachments from the 29th Native Infantry. We had, besides this, a well-armed civil gaol guard, who furnished the necessary guards at the civil officers' houses. Their strength was probably about a hundred men, but I do not remember exactly. Throughout the district was scattered the ordinary police force, which was amply sufficient for repressive purposes in times of peace. At Roorkie, in the Saharunpore district, and twenty-five miles distant from the town of Saharunpore, independently of the canal establishments, was the head-quarters of the sappers and miners, which at a very early date became only a source of anxiety.

In this position, then, with nearly a million of inhabitants in the district and a large Mahomedan population to control, were we launched into a rebellion where for long our only really reliable force consisted of a few gentlemen, canal overseers and clerks, distributed between the stations of Saharunpore and Roorkie. But the safety of Saharunpore during the revolt affected more than itself. Without taking into consideration the enormous loss that would have been entailed on Government from the destruction of the extensive canal workshops, aqueducts, engineers' college, &c., with loss of the treasure and magnificent stud, it was, politically speaking of the utmost importance that the Saharunpore district should be successfully held during the revolt. The army before Delhi was largely supplied from the canal establishments of Roorkie and other parts of the district with men and materials for forwarding the siege,* and the important services rendered by these men are amongst the peculiarities, or rather contradictions, everywhere presenting themselves during the revolt, many of their villages and relations being in open arms against the Government. Again, from the Saharunpore district were forwarded the supplies both of provisions and money, without which the hill stations of Mussouree and Landour, with their helpless occupants, chiefly composed of women and children, or, what was worse, old women in uniforms, might have been in no enviable position.

* Before the end of June, one party of 600 Beldars collected in this district took their departure to serve as pioneers before Delhi.

CHAPTER II.

The Hurdwar fair in 1857, immediately preceding the revolt—The pleasant retreat of Kunkul—Magisterial duties among the native chiefs—The fair broken up by cholera—Return through the Deyrah Dhoon towards Saharunpore — Captain H—— summoned to Umballah—Reports of intended risings of frequent occurrence previous to 1857—First rumours of an outbreak at Meeruth—Our postal communications interrupted—News of the Delhi outbreak—Singular question mooted—Resolve to hold out—Removal of the ladies from Saharunpore to the Himalayas — Defection of W—— and X—— — Total want of spirit in Meeruth and consideration for those in out districts—Europeans in Saharunpore, uniting, live in one house —We establish regular watches—A party of Europeans protected by villagers—Their removal into Saharunpore—Well-considered reward—Constant false alarms of attack—Approach of two companies of the sappers and miners—Our precautions to pass them through Saharunpore—Their mutinous conduct and return to Roorkie—Gallantry of Lieut. B—— W—— —Desertion of two of our party—Safe for the present.

In April, 1857, I had been to Hurdwar, to take charge of a rather well-known and extensive religious fair annually held in that locality, and lasting generally about a fortnight. The position of Hurdwar is well selected for this purpose; and being the point where the most sacred of Indian rivers issues from the hills, it has naturally become the resort of pilgrims. At this spot, surrounded by lofty snow-clad mountains, the broad crystal stream of the as yet unpolluted Ganges is launched into life amidst scenery of more than ordinary beauty. The geometrical perfection of the Hindoo temples, mingled with the picturesque abodes of the priesthood, generally constructed of a light-coloured sand-stone, hardly diminish the beauties here lavished by nature with so prodigal a hand, while they agreeably harmonize with the associations invariably called to mind when viewing this spot, sanctified in the eyes of a hundred and fifty millions of the human race by the traditions of upwards of two thousand years. To most of the race, indeed, it forms an ambition once in their lives to visit this locality, or, better still, to die here, and become directly incorporated with the essence of the universe. It is owing to the influence of this feeling that Kunkul, situated on the Ganges, some three miles below Hurdwar, has been adorned with many costly edifices, erected by pious rajahs, chiefs, and wealthy merchants, who, becoming weary of the troubles of life, have wandered far away from their birth-places,—in some instances, many hundreds of miles,—and here made themselves a home, where they are not only assured of present quiet, but may enjoy as they can the certain prospect of a peaceful and happy end.

The gallant little Sirmouree Battalion was the regiment sent to assist me in the maintenance of order at Hurdwar during the religious festival, or bathing-match, as it might be termed. A large party of officers from different parts of the country had also assembled here to witness the sight, purchase horses, or join in tiger-hunts. All was health and hope, and this a recognized holiday. I was probably the only one in the place actually hard at work, police and magisterial duties being combined with that of allotting encamping grounds to the different Seikh and Central Indian nobles, with their large armed bands, the disarming of whose retainers before permitting an entrance into the fair, though absolutely necessary for the maintenance of order, is always a sore subject with these rough customers, whose native pride or sense of dignity induces a morbid sensibility invariably on the look out for insults.

Little, I am certain, did any man there, even amongst the natives involved in the plot, dream of the wild storm about to burst over us. The rule of Company Bahador seemed secure enough, when native princes willingly surrendered their arms at the bidding of a soobahdar's party stationed at each entrance to the fair; and, though most of the Europeans there assembled were subsequently killed, they were not the only victims to the surprise—in all probability, many peaceful natives shared in the same fate, being overtaken in the storm before they managed to regain their homes. First, I ought to record, they suffered from a disaster of another kind.

Towards the end of April, cholera broke out in the fair, causing much consternation, and some loss of life. The fair broke up suddenly, and the people at once scattered, carrying the disease with them to the Punjaub, the hills, and all over the surrounding country.

There being no further necessity for my presence at Hurdwar, while my camp was returning to Saharunpore, taking a few elephants, I indulged myself, in company with some friends, in a short shooting trip into the Deyrah Dhoon; and when returning through the forests of my own district with Captain H——n, of the 9th Lancers (afterwards killed, poor fellow! at Lucknow), he received a note, recommending him to return to his regiment, as there were threatenings of disturbances at Umballah. At once, he rode across country to his own station, some hundred miles distant, and I returned to Saharunpore, looking forward with pleasure in the approaching great heat to the shelter of a house, little dreaming how brief the repose would be.

On my arrival, all were discussing the mutinous state of the native army, that fact being indubitable, though most were incredulous of all its dread reality. Being government servants, we trusted that the Government would act promptly, and that it was probably up to the mark; nor is this to be wondered at, as even during my short residence of from nine to ten years in India, had reports of apparently a more formidable nature, *i.e.*, of a Mahomedan religious war, been widely circulated, and yet had blown over without results.

Previous to the 15th of May, we had for several days been rather anxious to discover what amount of truth there might be in the native rumours prevailing in the city of Saharunpore regarding the outbreak at Meeruth, only seventy miles distant. Our usual posts from the south did not appear; so that, in the absence of either public or private communications, we knew not what to think of the state of affairs. The continued silence was hardly a good omen, for though the daily district police reports proved that all within the confines of our own district remained quiet, we naturally concluded that the peasantry in the neighbouring district must have joined the mutineers, or our communications would not have been interrupted. Being aware, however, of the existence of a large European force at Meeruth, we concluded that the contest, though clearly of a serious nature, must have been brief and decisive. Still, most of the few Europeans at Saharunpore, being married, on ascertaining the complexion of the outbreak, were naturally very anxious regarding the safety of their wives and children, there being no European troops nearer than the mutinous stations of Umballah and Meeruth. During this period of uncertainty, when speaking to several would-be-well-disposed natives, who, it was easy to observe, visited me more with the view of extracting than of furnishing information, I was much struck with their evident satisfaction in the generally unfavourable nature of the news, and with the promise of misfortune to the English.

By the evening of the 14th of May, we had received full particulars of the Meeruth outbreak; so that we were tolerably well prepared for the more threatening intelligence received on the evening of the 15th, from which it was clear the genius of the revolt aimed at nothing less than uprooting every vestige of the English race and civilization; nor was any fertility of imagination requisite to realize at a glance how precarious our position had become. While at office, engaged in my magisterial duties on that date, a horse-messenger brought a note from S——, requesting my immediate attendance at his house. I instantly drove off, and, when crossing the bridge, C—— met me, much excited. He informed me that worse news had been received, but that he had not heard the particulars. On reaching my destination, T——, S——, and Lieutenant B——w, were seated together, anxiously discussing some subject. On observing me enter, Lieutenant B——w jumped up and insisted that a simple statement of facts, with no opinions, should be given. The semi-official account of the Delhi outbreak was then read, including a statement of the general mutinous tone of the whole army. This completed, I was requested to vote whether the station should be held or not. The news surprised me less than this proposal, our treasury guard having as yet been guilty of no overt act of mutiny; and my decision was heartily welcomed by Lieutenant B——w, and the vote for holding on was declared carried. Seeing the necessity of having our action unfettered, it was determined that the ladies and children should at once be removed to Mussouree, while the northern road continued open. This being agreed to, Lieutenant B——w and myself drove off to prepare several of the married members of our community for instant action. Impressing the horses of absentees with our own, relays of horses were rapidly laid out to the Mohun Pass of the Sewalik range; but this being found insufficient for all, palkees and bearers were found by some. One family not possessing the means of removing all their children, I drove two of them, with their nurse, thirty miles to a staging bungalow on the road, and returned immediately to the station of Saharunpore, my two buggy horses dead beat, as, previous to this trip, they had been working hard the whole day, when I was engaged in visiting the various houses, with the view of accelerating our movements. This sudden call for exertion, when, likewise, the heat was so intense, must have been a severe trial to some of the ladies, who were far from well.

The first defection from our small party took place on this day; two gentlemen, W—— and X——, under the pretext of accompanying their wives to the hills, taking their departure and not returning. On the 15th of May we also received intimation of the mutiny of the treasury guard at Mozuffurnugur, and escape of the magistrates, Messrs. Grant and Berford, partly through the assistance of the sayuds of that place. The Rajah of Putteealah was, at the same time, reported to have seized many of this treasury guard, a step which we all considered a very important indication of the inclination of the Seikhs. The southern portion of our district was now, too, becoming covered with armed bands; one thanahdar, or chief police officer of a county, being obliged to abandon his post. Our communications were also constantly closed, though at times spasmodically open. Nevertheless, matters still looked well enough in the town of Saharunpore itself, as the sepoy treasury guard, our greatest cause of anxiety, continued true to their duty.

About this time T—— received a semi-official note from a man in high position at Meeruth, informing us, with the usual periphrasis, "that we should be happy to learn, &c., that Meeruth was actually holding its own against the enemy," the whole letter illustrating the universal want of spirit existing in Meeruth during the early days of the revolt. Meeruth, be it observed, was garrisoned by some 2,000 European soldiers. It was the only position in the North-West where more than a third of that number could be assembled, and that third even only existed at two places, Agra and Lucknow.

The vigour supposed co-existent with military dictation was here a phantom, and our respect for the dignitaries of Meeruth was hardly increased by a letter which, independently of its timidity, illustrated the general want of consideration for those really in dangerous positions. We had before noticed this, and we knew its result at Mozuffurnugur, where the miserable and imminently dangerous position of the two civilians in that district, lying between ourselves and Meeruth, had originated entirely in this feebleness. We knew that the military authorities had positively refused to send even fifty Europeans to secure the treasure and revenue of that district, in mortal alarm of weakening themselves too seriously, a policy which might have answered in the days of Lord Clyde, but which, had it prevailed generally at this period of the revolt, would have driven us out of the country.

It was difficult at first to discover what alarmed and paralysed Meeruth, for no sepoys existed nearer than Delhi, which place was separated from them by two rivers. We simpletons had, however, forgotten the Goojurs,* a horrible enough name doubtless, but an enemy whom solitary Europeans with twenty or

* See Dunlop's *Kakee Russala.*

fifty doubtfully loyal sepoys or troopers, were scattering to the winds in the surrounding out-districts. Not till the Kakee Russala was formed, composed chiefly of a few civilians and officers, thrown out of employ by the outbreak, did anarchy in the Meeruth district become extinguished, and the English name cease to be a contempt amongst the natives.

On the 19th of May, seeing that combination for mutual protection was necessary, we all united and lived in one house, making a division of horses, arms, &c., amongst those not possessing them. When we first called together the clerks and Eurasians to announce our determination of living in one house, I was astonished to find some of them refuse the offer of joining with us. We let them, however, take their own way, and, as anticipated, they changed their minds in a day or so, when they only seemed too glad to avail themselves of the offer. At the time, I could not divine their motives in selecting to live alone in isolated positions, as all the houses at Saharunpore were surrounded by extensive grounds; and, though there were few European residents, we were separated, in some instances, by more than a mile from each other. It afterwards came out, that the men considered living with us might interfere with their intention of eventually seeking safety by hiding themselves—a course which would probably have insured their destruction, had we been obliged to abandon the station, as subsequent judicial investigations in various parts of the country proved to me that not a single European or Eurasian was in hiding in any part of the country whose concealment had not become a notorious fact. In cases where such were preserved, it was almost entirely in consequence, not of the direct power of any particular zemindar in assembling a large body of retainers, but of his influence with his caste, or, through his connections, over a considerable tract of country. Even though the majority of the members of his caste or relations might have acted differently in their treatment of the European, if placed in his position, still their kinsman having made a resolute stand in any particular line of conduct, it became a Hindustani point of honour to support him. The knowledge of the existence of this clannish feeling often prevented rebel leaders from pressing too hard for the surrender of refugees, and the dread of an outburst of this partisanship has frequently prevented their interfering, where such a communion of sentiments had probably no existence at all.

It was about this date, the 18th or 20th of May, that Lieutenant H——e, of the Engineers, then in charge of a portion of the Eastern Jumna Canal, found himself, when encamped in the vicinity of two canal sergeants,* with their wives and families, overtaken by the rebellion on the borders of the

* Soldiers employed as superintendents of small divisions of the canals.

Mozuffurnugur district, some thirty miles distant. In that district British authority had almost ceased to exist, and was but feebly pulsating in the southern portion of our own, bordering on Mozuffurnugur. Lieutenant H——e, though he could himself have easily escaped by riding into Saharunpore, preferred linking his fortunes with the sergeants and their helpless families. Though the whole surrounding country was in a state of the most complete anarchy, this party fortunately found themselves in a village, forming one of a rather powerful brotherhood, who had always previously maintained constant feuds with the villagers then in rebellion. This village assembled their brethren, and declared in solemn conclave that the Europeans must be protected; and they kept their word, until Lieutenant B——w, collecting a sufficient number of elephants to make a rapid and unexpected march, managed, with his usual dashing gallantry, to bring the whole party into Saharunpore, before those in the rebel tract had even heard of his advent. These villages have since been rewarded through the Canal Department by a free grant in perpetuity of all water required for irrigational purposes from the Eastern Jumna Canal. This amounts to a considerable sum, and to these cultivators is about the most valuable and acceptable consideration that could be offered. The exemption, moreover, from the payment of all water dues as a recognition of their loyalty, while their neighbours continue to pay, is about as politic a reminder of the results of loyalty as could well be devised.

From the 20th of May, repeated alarms of intended attacks, continual discharge of fire-arms in the city and neighbourhood, with a total want of confidence in the natives round us, had resulted in the formation of regular watches, the members of which were wearied out by constant patrolling and sleepless nights, being numerically too weak to relieve each other properly. This apology for reliefs was, moreover, constantly upset by a universal call to arms.

As a pleasant addition to our anxieties we had received a formal notice that two companies of sappers and miners were to pass through Saharunpore on the morning of the 20th. This we had known for several days, and in the ordinary course of things, it was a very natural circumstance; but on the night of the 19th, we received an express warning us that the main body had mutinied at Meeruth, killing their commanding officer. We were very anxious to keep this a secret, but one of our party, in a desponding humour to which he was at times a victim, mentioned it to the tuhseeldar and other loyal natives, with the hope, we may presume, of obtaining their sympathy. Before daylight in the early morning, this mistake had been anxiously discussed by Lieutenant B——w and myself, and we agreed that some plausible excuse must be obtained for passing this infected body of men through the station in a hurried manner, so as to prevent their communicating with the detachment of the 29th Native Infantry forming our treasury guard, as also to save the lives of the two young inexperienced officers in charge of the detachment. To accomplish this, we determined to remove the provisions always collected by the civil authorities for troops marching through a district, from the usual encamping ground to a garden two miles on the other side of the city. Thus we expected to place the city between us before they could learn how the main body had acted at Meeruth. Lieutenant B——w, who was acquainted with the officers, gallantly proposed to ride out and meet the party some two miles beyond the station, and, if possible, quietly separate the officers in question from their men.

The preceding arrangements were all completed at daylight. Lieutenant B——w had left on his mission, and the necessary orders for removing the provisions had been issued. The rest of us (five I think) were seated in the verandah, debating on the probable result of our manœuvre, which for the time was important enough, as our lives seemed to depend considerably upon it, for we could not but be aware that the sepoys would at once suspect that something was wrong, when marched past the usual camping ground. Thus, hour after hour passed, and yet no Lieutenant B——w returned. Our solicitude, chiefly on his account, became great; at last we determined to commence breakfast, but two of our number, Y—— and Z——, who had, unknown to the rest of our party, prepared their horses, announced their intention of making for the hills, and they actually departed without their breakfast on a seventy-miles ride, with no very great share of our respect, as the desertion of men in their position would, we felt, exercise a most pernicious influence on the native mind.

After our deserters had gone, and we were breakfasting in silence, Lieutenant B——w, to our delight, reappeared. He had ridden out some four or five miles, and after a long delay, had returned, unable to discover anything that could account for the non-appearance of the sappers, or any particulars of their conduct. The fate of the two young officers was now the anxious question, but we had little time to think of them, and later in the day we ascertained that information of the mutiny of their regiment had reached the sappers. Instead, however, of breaking out at once, they informed their officers that they must accompany the detachment back to Roorkie to ascertain the truth of the report, so back they marched peaceably enough. Thus ended one short period of uncertainty. With bad luck, the district at any rate would have been lost.

CHAPTER III.

Commencement of an offensive line of action—Demonstrations against the rebel villages—Trip to the northern portion of the district—Capture of marauders—Loyalty of Deedar Singh and the Kheree zemindars—Seizure of rebel zemindars—The Bunjarahs of the Saharunpore district—Effect of the outbreak on this portion of the district—Joined by a party of Europeans in the Mohun Pass—Return to Saharunpore—Reinforcements from the Punjaub, and their value—Again leave Saharunpore, accompanied by a small force—Arrival at Deobund and reception there—Description of Deobund—State of the country in its neighbourhood—Attack made on a russaldar's party—Zemindars of the offending villages summoned—They arm to resist—We attack the villages—Difficulties attending our decision on this step—Sudden change that had come over these villages—The Khatah Rajpoots' reasons for not attacking them at once.

The events detailed in the preceding chapters had kept us in a painful state of suspense without affording the opportunity of decisive action. The little news that we obtained was also provokingly uncertain, as the roads to the south became daily less secure, being infested by parties of armed villagers incited by mutineers and escaped convicts, while the people evidently appreciated the importance to us of authentic information, and acted accordingly, The time was approaching, however, when it behoved us to adopt active measures for our preservation.

A few days preceding the 23rd of May, we ascertained that several of the larger villages in the neighbourhood had combined to attack us. On a fortunate suggestion we determined not to permit the rebels to select the most favourable opportunity for an attack, but, weak as we were, to assume the offensive; especially as this course would also test the fidelity of the sepoys of the 29th. The soobahdar in command of the treasury guard, after making some slight objections, gave us twenty men, and half our number, well mounted and armed, accompanied them, as horse, on the mornings of the 21st and 22nd, to attack the rebel villages. On our approach, the villagers generally retired and dispersed themselves, without a shot being fired. On one occasion we got hold of a body of armed men, drawn up to oppose us, but too weak to keep our prisoners after disarming them, we released the majority, first giving them a sound thrashing. Once, indeed, an excitable canal sergeant excited my indignation by firing at a man, but no harm was done. Both parties were, in fact, astonished at the novelty of their relative positions; and neither wished to commit themselves, on the one side, to overmuch severity, or, on the other, to flat rebellion. Each half anticipated a speedy solution of existing difficulties in the upshot of circumstances. These trips had the desired effect of clearing for a time the horizon in our immediate neighbourhood; but our communications, a vital point, continued in a very uncertain condition.

As the difficulties on the northern road were confined to our own district, it was determined to clear it. Here glaring atrocities had been committed; for, not being yet thoroughly broken in to the lively features of the revolt, we still considered them such, though a month later I would hardly have paused in reading the police officer's report of these natural events, the absence of which, in the daily reports, might have induced the suspicion that the police officer had either fraternized with the marauders or was doing the thing entirely on his own account. In one of these cases, certain Cashmerees, in charge of a valuable caravan, were, when passing through the Sewalik range, all either killed or wounded by the Bunjarahs. It was evident that British authority must soon become a mere name in this hilly locality were the criminals not punished at once.

Accordingly, on the morning of the 23rd of May, I started with twenty Foujdaree sowars (mounted police) to clear the Mohun road. Hardly ten miles from Saharunpore, we had the luck to fall upon men in the act of plundering our mail; and shortly after secured a band of twenty-six men, with a large amount of plundered property belonging to travellers or villages near the road. These prisoners, in consequence of the utter prostration of our civil power, I was obliged to hand over to certain zemindars of

Harowra, known to me in the neighbourhood, who furnished the necessary guard, and forwarded them in safety to Saharunpore. I then rode on to Kheree with the sowars and my companion, Mr. Hyde, a clerk in the judge's office. Here it struck me that it would never do to attempt the seizure of the Gokulwalla zemindars in their own village with horsemen alone, as in case of resistance my twenty horse would be useless amongst houses and walls. My only alternative was to test the loyalty of the neighbouring zemindars, with whom I had some previous acquaintance. I therefore summoned the zemindars of Kheree and a certain Deedar Singh. The latter was the feudal chief of a considerable portion of the Bunjarahs, who, in this part of the district, are the descendants of a tribe of Punjaub Bunjarahs, who had been tempted to emigrate, during the reigns of the last two Mahomedan emperors, from the Punjaub to this well-watered and grassy locality, so well suited to their herds of cattle.

Deedar Singh, naturally very retiring in manner, was a powerfully-built young man, with a handsome, though almost too mild, countenance, very devoid of expression. After some conversation, he and the Kheree zemindars promised to assist me with as many armed retainers as they could collect before night, though I kept them in ignorance as to the place I intended to attack. We marshalled our force a little before midnight, when I found Deedar Singh had brought about a hundred men, and the Kheree zemindars some fifty more, a considerable number of whom were well armed. Starting shortly after midnight, we managed to surround the village of Gokulwalla by day-dawn, when the offending zemindars were apprehended without resistance. The zemindars of Kheree being poor men, and knowing it would please them, I doubled the strength of all the police stations by enlisting their men, and we never subsequently received any trouble from this part of the district. This, however, might be chiefly attributed to its being a thinly-peopled tract, cut up by strips of jungle, and separated from the dangerously revolutionary portions of the district by the station of Saharunpore.

This was the first occasion on which I had proceeded to any distance from the town of Saharunpore since the outbreak, and I was much struck by the change that event had already produced. We were now traversing the high road from the North-West Provinces to the Deyrah Dhoon and the Himalayas. In ordinary times, at this season of the year, this road is invariably crowded to excess with an extensive traffic, and travellers, European and native. Now, except a few bands of armed men, travelling in company for mutual protection, not a soul was to be seen, the only pleasing feature in the solitary aspect of the country being the friendliness of the zemindars located on the borders of the forest, who seemed to me—as far as it is possible to unriddle natives from appearances—the most actively loyal (interest rendered many passively so) of any it was my lot to meet during the mutinies. They must have seen clearly enough, that by refusing their small contingents, I should have been powerless; for the horse police who accompanied me were poorly armed, utter curs at heart, and would, I am certain, have bolted on the very first shot from a Bunjarah's dreaded matchlock.

After forwarding to Saharunpore the prisoners taken at Gokulwalla, I rode on with my friend, Mr. Hyde, to look after the passes through the Sewaliks. At Mohun, the entrance to a pass through the Sewalik range—some twenty or thirty miles from the Mussouree hill station—was a small staging bungalow, which now became my head-quarters. About 11 A.M., on the 24th, a report was brought in that an armed party was descending the pass, which caused us to turn out; but we soon discovered that the strangers consisted of European officers returning from leave in the hills, who, being anxious to join their regiments or posts, had united for mutual protection. The refugees from our own station having been laughed at till they were shamed into a descent, had mustered courage enough to join this party. The following morning they all accompanied me from Kheree to Saharunpore, my return there with the mounted police being necessary, that we might be enabled to muster as strong as circumstances would admit of near the city during the Eed of the Mahomedans.

For some time, since comprehending the alarm existing at Meeruth, we had turned our eyes to the Punjaub, where the authorities had been pressed to send us any slight assistance in their power. On reaching Saharunpore, we found that two squadrons of the 4th Native Lancers, with several companies of the 5th Native Infantry, had marched in from Umballah. The three European officers who accompanied this force, proved our chief reinforcement, as the men under their command had already shown that they could not be trusted. On the whole, the fresh arrivals did not add much to our sense of security; yet those who took an interest in the safety of the district were glad to see the 4th and 5th. In our position they were actually reinforcements. We were playing a game of brag; the holder of the worst hand might yet be the winner. A chance existed of the native troops holding out long enough to subdue the rebellious villages, which would otherwise swamp us, and the sepoys might not be prepared to mutiny, and shoot us down, till some fortunate turn in the chapter of incidents, such as the fall of Delhi or advance of Europeans from Cawnpore—for still a lingering hope existed in those directions—might alter the positions of both parties, and render the native troops loyal, or make us independent of them. We felt that we must, in fact, hold on at all risks, and hope for the best, as Meeruth, our legitimate head-quarters, was still too much alarmed to spare us even fifty Europeans, which, with a reasonably intelligent officer in command, would have placed the representatives of government authority—or, what was probably more valuable, the government treasure and stud—in a position of absolute security.

On the 26th of May, the day after my return from the north, though worn by daily exposure to the full blaze of an Indian May sun, I found it again necessary to take to the saddle, mounting one of those trusty horses, two of which, poor creatures, died from fatigue in the close of the year, at a time when they ceased to be of so great importance to me, though their loss was felt as that of old and well-tried friends. The state of the southern portion of the district and the presence of shaky reinforcements, whose attention it was important to divert from passing events, all induced immediate action. Accompanied by a portion of the 4th Lancers, with Captain W——d in command, and a few of the 29th Native Infantry, besides some mounted police, we started in the direction of Deobund. On the march we were joined by an officer, Major W——s, anxious to take advantage of our escort so far on his road to Meeruth, and as he was known to some of the men in the 29th Native Infantry, the regiment to which he belonged, I requested him to remain a day or two with us, deeming his presence with them an advantage, should there be fighting. To this he willingly consented.

Early on the morning of the 27th May we neared our destination. On approaching Deobund, all the moneyed classes of the city, or those who had anything to lose by a disturbance, came out a considerable distance on the road and gave us a hearty welcome as their deliverers, having been evidently much alarmed by the threatening state of the country around. They next insisted on my parading with them through certain of the principal streets, with the view of restoring confidence, and inducing the shopkeepers to open their shops. With the exception of the government servants, however, I observed few or no Mahomedans amongst this gathering or in the streets.

Deobund is an ancient and populous Hindoo town, though now a considerable Mahomedan population have taken up their abode there. It is situated on the main line of road between Meeruth, Saharunpore, and the Punjaub, and surrounded by extensive groves, embedded in which are some much-venerated Hindoo shrines. In the grounds surrounding one of the largest of these temples is the most extensive collection of Suttee monuments that I have ever met with. They are closely packed together amongst some fine old trees, and are generally about the size of monuments erected in our own burial-grounds.

But their outlandish shapes and sombre aspect render them fitting representatives of the demoniacal rites they record. Even animals would seem to be impressed with the strangeness of the locality, as on one occasion I observed that the horses of a party who were visiting the place seemed to become much alarmed on discovering that they were surrounded by these memorials of barbarism. The monuments, however, are now fast crumbling to pieces, and will hardly outlive the creed they represent, of which this revolt has been the death-knell, for Christianity has already commenced a new and vigorous existence amongst the ruins of its churches and missions.

On arriving at Deobund, I at once commenced investigations, with the view of discovering the culprits in several daring outrages committed in the neighbourhood. It turned out that whole villages, not individuals, were at fault. In one case, a russaldar (native officer of cavalry), having just been placed on the pension list in the Punjaub, was travelling to his home with several of his comrades and their families. Belonging to the Irregular Cavalry, whose arms are their own property, all were well armed, so might be considered rather a formidable party. Three villages united to attack them, and, after the infliction of some severe wounds, their property being secured, the whole party were marched back to the neighbourhood of Deobund, where men and women, after being stripped, were dismissed. I at once issued notices to the zemindars of the offending villages to attend and answer the charges brought against them. Before long, however, the anticipated reply came in, that the zemindars had not the slightest intention of appearing, but had despatched horsemen in all directions, with the view of collecting their clansmen to oppose us. It was clear they must be attacked at once, before their expected reinforcements would arrive; for, small as our force was, we were obliged to diminish it still further by leaving a guard over our camp. Prior to attacking these villages, it being evident that this would be our first serious passage of arms, the decision how to act, and that at once, was, at first, to an officer inexperienced in such positions, trying in the extreme. Civil authority being still supposed to be supreme, the responsibility of failure would be borne by the civil officer alone. An experienced military man, Major W——s, then in camp, strenuously advised, considering our small force and the reported strength of the enemy, that the attack should not be attempted without reinforcements. But the offensive, mild as it was, had hitherto been successful, and of reinforcements there was no hope. Retreat, without striking a blow, as an acknowledgment of weakness, would at once raise a wavering and formidable population. My adviser, moreover, though probably correct in a military point of view, looked only to immediate consequences; for as he would be in Meeruth with an European garrison in a few days, my deep interest in the ultimate results could not actuate him. Whatever, therefore, the disagreeable responsibility of my position in acting contrary to such advice, it seemed to me that the duty was imperative. Retreat, by increasing their distrust, might raise our own force against us as well as the country.

The officer, Captain W——d, in command of the Lancers, being willing to assume his portion of the risks, and uphold my decision, I determined to consider Major W——s in his true position, as only a volunteer, and instant action was determined upon. The mind seems but gradually to become inured to scenes of violence, and to accept, without reserve, the responsibilities of action in doubtful positions. Frequently, after the constant recurrence of similar scenes, when, hardened by circumstances, I was able to scan with complacency the probable results of such a decision, have I looked back with wonder at my anxious feelings when advancing on this occasion. I had, as it were, staked the safety of a large district, when so peremptorily insisting on the attack being made against the advice of an old soldier. Any failure would be justly visited upon me; so that, on the march, a lingering hope remained that our rapid advance might intimidate the enemy into submission or flight. All along I half dreaded that Major W——s' spies (Major W——s was, I think, at that time superintendent of cantonment police in the North-West Provinces), a few of whom accompanied him, and had been sent to gather information, might be more correct in their exaggerated statements than my police, whose reports, after all, turned out very near the truth.

When nearing the refractory villages, Captain W——d, with the cavalry, had gone on in advance to reconnoitre. Though fully determined to confront all opposition, the firing in the direction of the cavalry, I must confess, rather surprised me. But this might be caused by our own party wishing to intimidate their opponents into submission. On coming up, however, any doubts as to what the firing really was, were rapidly solved by our reception from a garden in our front. I did not expect it would come to this, and certainly hoped it would not. Some six weeks earlier in the season, these villages had been in my beat when working at the revenue settlement; and at that time all interested in the land, whether rich or poor, crowded round me in anxious discussion, when wandering over their lands alone and unarmed. They were then only too painfully pressing in their anxiety to show me every attention, and myself equally desirous to sift the truth for their benefit, as well as that of the Government; troops might mutiny, but I could hardly realize this rapid change amongst peaceful villagers.

In consequence of the position taken up by the villagers amongst groves and gardens, where cavalry, of which our force almost entirely consisted, was useless, we stood aloof for some time discussing matters, while Captain W——d was instructing me in his plans. This emboldened the villagers, who advanced a short distance into the open, which soon terminated our difficulties. It was determined that our twenty sepoys should advance first, and Captain W——d was to charge in line as we got to close quarters, so as to give our force the most imposing appearance circumstances would admit of. Here Major W——s, who had up to this moment continued strenuously remonstrating against the attack, now, with generous gallantry, waiving all personal considerations, placed himself at the head of his own men, when our small band advanced with a rush, and Captain W——d, shortly charging, scattered the rabble: the loss on our side being one mounted policeman, who had cautiously kept far to the rear, the only dangerous position; the villagers, as usual in their excitement, firing high and injuring none near them. A few of the villagers were killed, and some made prisoners; the wounded being sent into the hospital at Saharunpore. A slightly amusing incident occurred near Baboopoor. Observing a few Lancers driving about a herd of women who had taken shelter under the bank of a stream, I proceeded to check this apparently unnecessary conduct. On remonstrating with them the troopers declared that armed men were hidden under the women's petticoats, and sure enough two great Goojurs thus secreted were shortly produced.

To the south-west of our encamping ground, Deobund, lay a turbulent and powerful tract, called the Khatah. To make this district feel our power, even in an isolated town or two, would, it seemed to me, tend for a time to keep the less powerful quiet. This was, therefore, my next point of attack, but a storm, accompanied by a deluge of rain, prevented our marching as intended, on the 28th, to strike the blow in the Khatah. On my declaring that this must be done, the officer of the 29th who had joined us at once left for Meeruth, resolved to wash his hands of complicity in my movements. But the experience of the previous day had not been totally lost sight of. It showed me clearly that the zemindars were one with the lower orders; that rebellion, not plunder alone, actuated the mass of the population; so the compulsory delay caused by the storm was actively employed in sifting out the actual extent of resistance intended to be carried out against us.

The Khatah and its Rajpoot race were well known to me. Here also I had been engaged in settlement duties a few months earlier during the cold season; an undulating, well-watered, and rather sandy tract, this is the finest horse district in Northern India, perhaps in the whole country. The horses of the Khatah

Rajpoots are good-tempered, large, and powerful, and they are the pride and chief object of endearment of this race. I knew, moreover, that this portion of the district had frequently risen in rebellion and defied our troops for several years after our first occupation of the country, and to a very late date had always given much trouble. Men and horses being good, this district could easily muster a body of horse, such as could not be found in a tract of the same extent in our provinces, whilst our former compromising policy had left their forts undemolished, and the country armed; for the mutinies alone would seem to have revealed the strength of an armed population. With our force, small though it was, my object was to attack the Khatah before rebellion had assumed an organized and concerted form. But the hearts of our men were not in the work. With a stout resistance, mutiny would also face us. By the evening the conclusion at which the departed officer had arrived seemed, after all, not to be despised, and our plans were changed.

CHAPTER IV.

Prudential notice sent to the Khatah zemindars—March to Nagul—Arrival of a gentleman from Saharunpore—Arrangements for attacking the rebels near Munglour—Our encampment at Nagul, and position amongst the sepoys—Supposed mutiny of the Nusseerees—Captain W——d's anxieties for the safety of his wife—The march—Necessity of concealing all plans even from natives in authority—Keenness of Hindustani perceptions—Their unaccountable impulses—Anecdote of a native convert to Christianity during the revolt—Distrust of the intentions of the British Government—Rebels retreat on our advance—Encampment at Kheree—Excitement amongst the 29th Native Infantry—A Brahmunee woman the agent of mutiny—The 29th demand revenge against an offending village—Our refusal and forced march into Saharunpore—The sepoys of the 29th Native Infantry—Mercenary character of the sepoys a hopeful feature in our future connection with India—Love of the old Company Bahador—Their wish to oppose the demon of mutiny—Inability to resist its inspiration—Caste combination in India—Caste the only religion in the North-West Provinces—Unaccountable conduct of the 29th Native Infantry—Reasons for our march into Saharunpore—Our calculations upset—The 5th Native Infantry evince a mutinous spirit on the march—Different results of exposure in the hot winds and the rainy season—Further indications of mutiny amongst the 5th Native Infantry—Oosman Khân of Belaspore; his advice and offer of protection—Oosman Khân and Deedar Singh become friends—Cease to be so on the fall of Delhi—The Mahomedan and Bunjarah—The 5th Native Infantry ordered to march—Their refusal—The men offered their discharge and arrears of pay—They seize their arms—Mutiny of the 5th Native Infantry—A loyal sepoy shoots a mutineer when attempting to intercept Captain W——d—Position of the Europeans during this mutiny

—Our rendezvous and guns—The mutineers retire—Our uncertainty as to the actual state of affairs—Conduct of the 29th Native Infantry during this mutiny—Their refusal to act—How far fortunate—Conduct of the loyal amongst the 5th Native Infantry—Providential escape of three Europeans—The 4th Lancers in pursuit—Our position after the mutiny—Excited state of the loyal sepoys—Remarkable fidelity of two of my servants during this outbreak.

HAVING determined to abandon the Khatah expedition, it seemed prudent to act on the assumption of the people's loyalty. Accordingly, I at once issued orders to the rebel zemindars of that tract, many of whom were personally known to me, to collect provisions in sufficient quantities to supply a force of double our present strength, as a hint that we might appear if circumstances necessitated it; a threat, indeed, that hardly required to be fulfilled, as the punishment inflicted on Baboopoor had the salutary effect of keeping them quiet for a couple of months, when I again visited the locality. At midnight we headed our small column in the opposite direction; arriving at Nagul, some twelve miles from Saharunpore, about ten in the morning.

Shortly after coming to our encamping ground, one of the party from Saharunpore, who had been warned of our approach, arrived. He brought with him what was then important to the most indifferent —the last news; but it was such a confused mass of disheartening matter, that it was a relief to learn that his object in coming was to inform us of a large gathering in the Munglour direction. In consequence of this, we made arrangements to meet each other at daybreak next morning at a point as near as possible to the head-quarters of the rebels; and, the enemy being reported strong, this gentleman was to reinforce us with all the remaining station force that could possibly be spared. He then returned to prepare, and, overcome by the oppressive heat, Captain W——d and myself lay down under the trees, rendered almost leafless by the hot winds, discussing together our chances of holding the country till our camp with the rear-guard made its appearance late in the afternoon; so late, indeed, that we began to suspect all had not gone right, and many an anxious eye we both turned on our loyal men now assembled in small groups all round us, and who still continued pointedly respectful. Only too much so in fact. There was no confidence on either side, though both parties endeavoured to appear utterly indifferent, and to keep up cheerful conversations. Both saw through the hollow sham.

Previously, in the morning, Captain W——d had received notice of the then supposed mutiny of the Nusseerees at Simla, and it was added that his wife, with some other ladies, had fled into the interior of the hills, no one knew where, probably none less than themselves. This was enough to try a less feeling and gentle nature than his. Already we distrusted every native, and a race defection was no novelty. To suggest to my friend the possibility of the safety of his wife seemed almost an unfeeling insult. If the Nusseerees had joined in the mutiny, as we then doubted not, we could hardly expect their own hill tribes not to side with them, and the cruelty of the hill races was pre-eminent even amongst the denizens of Hindustan. If one portion of the hills were in revolt, the flame would rapidly spread, when the fate of the ladies in the different hill stations would exceed in horror anything that we had yet heard of.

After strolling amongst and conversing with the sepoys in the evening, I was again much struck with their anxious respectfulness, not unmingled with a sorrowful expression of sympathy. We now retired to our tent, guarded by the faithful sepoys. Both had long continued almost silent; and it was with pleasure my assent was given, when Captain W——d proposed reading some portion of the sacred Scripture before attempting to sleep, for we could not but feel how entirely all the few scattered Europeans in Northern India must depend upon the will of One more powerful than themselves.

With the advancing hours of night, hardly had the hot winds moderated sufficiently to render sleep a possibility and a relief, than the usual midnight bugle summoned us to mount, and off we tramped in the hot darkness, men and horses equally weary and wayworn, stumbling over stumps or into deep ruts. All were wrapped in that oppressive unnatural silence that I have since often felt as peculiar to those times, and rarely was it interrupted, except when roused from our reveries by the occasional return of troopers from the advanced guard. In this line of country I was unacquainted with the cross roads, or rather paths. It consequently became necessary to beat up for guides, and the whole country for miles anticipated our plans. Unless on the grand lines of road, secrecy in the movements of a force not accompanied by a European who knows the country well, is almost an impossibility. It is then necessary to procure guides for a particular line of country, the enemy is at once informed, and every movement anticipated. If one native, whatever his position, knows your plans, secrecy is at an end.

The Hindustanis, however amenable to the charge of treachery and cowardice, and though themselves totally wanting where boldness of action is necessary, are extremely quick in perceiving, and appreciate to the full, this better quality in others; at the same time, their impulses are extravagant beyond what any unacquainted with the facts would deem possible in so clever a race. In the ordinary transactions of native life, constantly brought to the notice of the civil officer, I have often observed instances of this. Let but a native, particularly of the north-western portions of the North-West Provinces, once form an impression, however wild, and he will rush into ruin, and blast all future prospects, as if they were not for a moment to be weighed in the balance with the gratification of a transient impulse. When ruin stares the native in the face, he sees clearly the absurdity of his course, he repines little, sits down quite complacently, thinks little more on the subject, puts it all down to the credit of *Khismut* (fate), and begins life again as if nothing had taken place.

As an example in point, I may mention the case of a native who at first seemed actually to rise above his race in his obstinate adherence to convictions, though these, as usual, were rather impulsively formed. It was in January, 1858, I believe, when encamped with Sir Thomas Seaton's force at Futtehgurh, that a native one day loudly demanded admittance to my tent. Permission being given, a man presented himself in a very excited state, declaring his wish to be made a Christian without a moment's delay. As my strange visitant appeared to be hardly in the possession of his senses,* and his request, in

* All fuckeers, devotees, &c., in the North-West Provinces drug themselves largely, and are one of the few classes who ever show that an extensive use of bungh or opium has been resorted to. All the Seikhs of the Punjaub, with the Jâts, Rajpoots, and other castes in the North-West Provinces and Central India, consume large quantities of opium, and yet in few parts of the world is it possible to see more healthy and finer races. Again, when I was at Chang-Chow and other places in the interior of China, with Padre Zerre, a Spanish Jesuit missionary, I constantly visited the opium shops; but neither there did I ever see, as the result of opium, anything approaching the degradation or ruin to be witnessed in enlightened Europe with its civilized drinks. Opium is, in every respect, more harmless, both to the recipient and his friends, particularly in a

the then state of the country, seemed at least peculiar, he was ordered to move out, but to return the next day to mention whether his sentiments had undergone any change, though at the time it was a mystery to me how the man had managed to pass through the European sentries. The prospect of ever seeing this gentleman again appeared but small, and the interview was at the time treated as an ordinary piece of native eccentricity hardly worthy of notice. The following day, however, my new acquaintance again presented himself, reiterating his original request, and being sober enough, and serious in his purpose, I was tempted to inquire into his history.

The name of the man was Prayag Dâs, and, originally of the poorer class of cultivators, he had become one of those numerous religious devotees constantly wandering along the banks of the Ganges. Many of these poor creatures pass exemplary lives, and have adopted the religious profession with the sincerely anxious desire to discover the Great Unknown. Subsequent inquiries showed that this man in particular was much respected throughout his own particular

tropical climate, than the wines or spirits of Europe. The claptrap philanthropists of Europe and America might possibly effect more good by initiating reform nearer their own homes, than by offering England rather interested lectures, it may be, on the demoralizing effects of opium. It is an acknowledged fact, that almost all races, particularly within the tropics, seek and require a stimulant of some kind, and it may be doubted whether, when eradicating opium, it would be easy to discover another stimulant which is morally and physically less injurious.

beat on the banks of the Ganges, where he was in the receipt of very considerable fees from those who worshipped or bathed in his neighbourhood. Some months after the revolt had banished all vestiges of English rule from Rohilkund, Prayag Dâs accidentally met an Eurasian, named John Peter. The Eurasian, like many other Christians who had escaped from the massacres at the first outbreak in that province, was wandering about in disguise, hunted from place to place by the adherents of Khan Bahador Khan, the rebel chief of Rohilkund. Prayag Dâs, in common with many of his class, actuated by no particular love for anything English, yet averse to the shedding of blood in any form, assisted in concealing Mr. John Peter, whose communications he managed to convey to Mr. J. C. Wilson's party, when that gentleman, formerly the judge of Moradabad, made his daring trip, almost unparalleled even in the Indian revolt, through the heart of a rebel country, and within a few miles of Ahmed Yar Khan's army, to rescue the various Europeans and Christians still alive in Rohilkund. It appeared that while Prayag Dâs was in Mr. John Peter's company, the latter had constantly conversed with him on the subject of Christianity. The impression thus left on his mind had proved so enduring, that now, on our reoccupation of the country, he had zealously come forward, and professed his wish to be made a Christian.

The man was evidently sincere, but all missionaries

formerly in the neighbourhood having been swept off by the revolt, he was offered means to enable him to reach the Deyrah Dhoon, where he could receive instruction. The Deyrah Dhoon was some 300 miles distant, with a disturbed, half-conquered country intervening, yet the persevering convert eventually found his way there to my friend Mr. Woodside, of the American mission, who, some ten or twelve months subsequently, sent him back to me. He was then offered employment in the Furruckabad gaol guard, where he would possess the important advantage of the company of other native Christians; but this, to my astonishment, he indignantly refused, insisting on being allowed to accompany my camp, and claiming a recognition from the Government, similar to that which had been awarded to other natives who had assisted Christians in the hour of danger. The reward looked for, I may observe, was a small portion of confiscated land which might enable him to earn a livelihood by returning to the occupation he had originally abandoned.

Both proposals might, under ordinary circumstances, be considered quite natural, but at this juncture they were attended with peculiar difficulties. The first demand I could not entertain for an instant, as, being at that time vested with power of life and death all over the North-West Provinces, the presence of this man in my camp might lead to endless misconceptions regarding the intentions of the British

Government, at a time when the people were more deeply suspicious of the policy of their conquerors than even during the excitement of the first outbreak; and, on the other hand, in the press of more important work, the allotment of land would take more time to arrange than could possibly be devoted to it. In short, Prayag Dâs was informed that he must accept for the present the appointment offered to him, on which he moved himself off, impulsive as usual, and greatly offended; possibly any explanation of reasons on my part may have been too brief for his taste, as I had enough in the shape of official duties to engage all my time.

The matter did not end here, as might be supposed. Some three months later, Prayag Dâs reappeared, and reported that, having found Mr. John Peter, that worthy old man had recommended him to accept the appointment. Probably, he had found it harder to obtain a livelihood than he anticipated, after the abandonment of his devotee's throne (*guddee**), and convinced at last that I could not otherwise assist him, he followed the advice of his friend and accepted the appointment. He thus experienced one of those lessons Hindustanis are eternally administering to themselves, the effects of which may not evaporate for some six or eight months. Before I left the country, Prayag Dâs,

* In India the devotee is not distinguished by his garb, as he rarely possesses any, but by his *guddee*, which signifies either a seat or a throne, and they love to apply the latter signification to it.

in great delight, announced to me his intention of marrying a native Christian girl, which will probably settle the question of his remaining a Christian, on which point I had before considerable misgivings.

Before daybreak on the 30th of May, we reached the rendezvous determined on the previous day; and, shortly after, we were joined by our friends from Saharunpore, with a reinforcement of two companies of the 5th Native Infantry, under Captain G——n. We now advanced several miles, scouring the country with the cavalry, but the enemy had disappeared; indeed, hardly a human being was to be seen. Under these circumstances, Captain W——d and myself, with the whole force, falling back a few miles, encamped at Kheree,* our Saharunpore friends riding and driving back to the station at once. The officer in command of the 5th Native Infantry remained with his regiment and with my party, but exposure to the sun had rendered him senseless, and thus he continued till late in the afternoon.

Hardly had we discussed a late dusty breakfast, when five or six of the 29th Native Infantry came forward very respectfully to inform us that one of their company was missing. I promised that some horse police should be sent to ascertain what had become of him, when the men went away quite contented; but even here we were haunted by emis-

* There are a number of towns called Kheree, or Khera, in the Saharunpore district, which often leads to considerable confusion.

saries of revolt. In about an hour the sepoys in a large body returned, very excited, to state that their brother in arms had been killed, and the body desecrated. The village, they insisted, must be punished. I told them that the police had as yet brought back no information to me, and asked how they had obtained theirs. A woman, they informed me, brought the news. The woman was summoned, who, before them, boldly enough entered into an account of the sepoy's death, with such trivial additions as invariably excite Hindoo prejudices. There was no mistaking her mission, and I longed to make an example of her at once; but our position forbade it, as she was a Brahmunee, and her sex, for the time, saved her. I placed her under a few police orderlies in front of the tent, and recommended the men to wait the return of the police. They left in the most threatening manner.

The police shortly returned with an account of how the sepoy (a Hindoo) had been killed by a Brahmun when plundering a small Hindoo temple, and that, the place having been fired, the body had been consumed. The sepoys were summoned, and the case put before them: they instantly demanded vengeance with the most violent gesticulations; they were at last firmly informed that it would not be permitted, and were ordered off. Their violence now changed to sullen determination, and they went away quietly. We had thus, to the more ignorant portion, clearly proved that all the lies circulated by those in rebellion had a foundation; we had insulted them by forbidding one of the most sacred duties inculcated by their religion. The body of their comrade could not be recovered, and we would not sanction revenge even on what might easily be brought under the catalogue of a rebellious village. We momentarily expected an explosion, but our horses, our only possible means of escape, could not be ordered without bringing matters to a crisis at once.

During these stormy discussions, our rifles being within grasp, a pale, childish-looking officer, just out from England, lying asleep beside me, worn out by fatigue, suggested the thought whether the men would respect his life more than ours. However, Captain W——d and myself determined that, though the men must be almost dead beat, a march, to engage their attention, had become an absolute necessity, if we hoped to keep Captain W——d's Lancers and the 5th disaffected. These troops had not previously met for a considerable time, and it was improbable that a combination had as yet taken place. The necessary orders were, therefore, issued. Captain G——n, of the 5th, was roused as much as possible, and, having recovered sufficiently to sit his horse, we all mounted. The start, we felt, would become the test of immediate mutiny. It became of importance that some men should lead off with willing obedience, and Captain W——d's Lancers certainly did not hesitate, nor the 5th, who followed. All passed off quietly, and the 29th, left to the charge of their native officers, brought up the rear. Little did I dream that these very men of the 29th would remain faithful almost to the fall of Delhi, whilst most of the others would be mutineers within little more than twenty-four hours.

This company of the 29th Native Infantry was a miniature illustration of the native army. They were all nearly of the same high castes, and from the same or neighbouring villages. Physically superior to the generality of Europeans, they were an extremely handsome set of men. All nearly were actuated by the same feelings of affection or revenge; they saw clearly that the comfort of themselves and families depended on their fidelity. They had no faith in their own race as paymasters, while the certainty of regular and high pay has been from the commencement of our rule one of the strongest, perhaps the only real inducement to fidelity amongst our native troops. It will be observed throughout the revolt of 1857, that one of the first demands made by the sepoys to the rebel chiefs was invariably an increased rate of pay, or their services would be transferred elsewhere; * and how utterly mercenary they

* In the course of subsequent investigations, in several parts of the country, papers came into my possession, showing that an attempt was made to induce the sepoys to remain, for the purpose of maintaining the authority of any particular rebel chief, in the part of the country where they happened to be located at the

were, even in revolt, and when fighting nominally for a patriotic cause, appears from the manner in which they at once deserted the colours of their rebel chiefs when money was not forthcoming, though the country people, in almost all instances, willingly supplied their wants. This, as I have before remarked, is one hopeful feature in calculating the chances of permanency in our rule over the country. With all this deep mercenary feeling, however, the sepoys, from long habit and custom, did actually love and reverence that, to them, incomprehensible power —the old Company Bahador. There was a charm in that great name, which had conquered and ruled with parental care two hundred millions of the human race, and they still wished to continue its honoured servants, for such they were and felt themselves to be, nor hitherto unjustly so.

Their hour had not yet come; but a mysterious demon, the Nemesis of lies, was wafting these misguided men of the 29th, with none the less unerring certainty, under the influence of the great spell. For the time they were determined to fight against mutiny, but the voice of the country—perhaps of their own villages, which is all in all to a native—was taunting them with their conduct already, in

time of the outbreak, by guaranteeing the Delhi standard of allowances, and in one or two instances, as at Mynporie, a still higher rate; but in this latter class of cases the security was evidently not considered good, the sepoys not being induced to remain.

opposition to that of their political caste and the will of the army. Unanimity of action in every political or social question, the flock of ignorants being led by the few, is almost the only point of honour known or acknowledged amongst the natives of India, and it is common to them all, whether barbers or soldiers, Hindoo or Mahomedan,—all combine with wonderful and tenacious unanimity. Our strikes in England, as depicted by Hugh Miller,* bear some analogy to this. Combination alone is the mainstay and secret of the maintenance of caste, and caste in the North-West Provinces is the only religion; few trouble themselves on any other point. When in health, the Hindustani of the North-West is far too independent to be led so blindly by the nose by priests as the miserable inhabitants of Lower Bengal or other portions of India. It was but natural then, in spite of some dark prejudices regarding the departed and their influence in this world, that all religion should resolve itself into a strict maintenance of caste, so flattering to the vanity of a vain race.†

* Of a strike in which Hugh Miller was engaged, he says, "It is the wilder spirits that dictate the conditions, and, pitching their demands high, they begin usually by enforcing acquiescence in them on the quieter and more moderate of their companions. They are tyrants to their fellows ere they come into collision with their masters."

† Caste punctilios are now and then varied by spirit and demon worship; thus, those who die of small-pox, or by being hanged, or women in child-birth, are condemned to wander as bhoots, or ghosts, for millions of years on the banks of certain large rivers, and to haunt their descendants from generation to generation.

In addition to its present quiet submission, this company also represented in itself many of those paradoxical peculiarities observable throughout the mutiny. The man who was most conspicuous in our discussions at the camping ground as violent and uncompromising in his gestures and language, was one of two men who refused to join in the mutiny of his company, when that event occurred. He was one of the sincere class over whom designing natives worked their wicked will; but before the fatal day arrived, he had his eyes opened, and time was given for reflection.

It might be thought that our decision to march at

The result being, that a misfortune, supposed to originate with these bhoots, now and then places something in the pockets of the Gungaputrs, sons of Ganges, or induces a woman to drown herself in the village well, to be revenged on her husband in the shape of an avenging bhoot. At times they also propitiate by offerings the demon of epidemics, occasionally, however, treating him rather harshly. Thus, in the Bolundshuhur district, in 1856, I remember some most serious affrays, the results of attempts to drive the dreaded cholera out of particular villages. The infected village would procure a black buffalo to represent the spirit of this scourge, covering him over with well-tarred torches; all not prostrated by the disease would, about midnight, well armed, attend the beast with lighted torches and their infernal music to the borders of an uninfected village. Here, lighting the torches tied over the already-excited animal, they would attempt to drive this fitting representation of their afflicting demon across the boundary into their neighbour's lands; but their neighbours are on the look out, and quite ready to receive them, so that serious affrays are the result. The women also follow the good example of their husbands, and get up small affrays of their own, by throwing furniture and domestic utensils into their neighbours' fields with the same view—that of getting rid of the cholera.

once into Saharunpore at such a moment was hardly politic, as endangering the safety of the station, but various considerations determined our course; chiefly, we considered, that we should be better able there to control the men on our ground in the station itself than in the district, while the troops themselves would probably have refused to march in any other direction. The 5th we thought tolerably staunch, and they were under positive orders to march back to Umballah, which gave a plausible colouring to a second long march on the same day. The 29th might, for a time, be partially controlled by the 5th, and the station would, under any circumstances, be lost if our force mutinied, for it was all that Saharunpore possessed.

On the march our calculations were again upset, as some of the 5th behaved most insolently to Captain G——n, this being the more significant, as he was, without doubt, a great favourite amongst his men, and possessed very considerable influence with them. Yet the 1st of June passed quietly; and great was the relief to find oneself in a house well protected from the scorching sun and hot winds. I may here remark that, though disagreeable, these winds are not actually unhealthy, if the protection of a house can be secured, and attendance in a crowded cutchery* is not necessary. Still, exposure to an Indian sun, during the prevalence of the hot winds, is more

* Cutchery, a magistrate's or collector's court.

immediately prostrating than during the rainy season, when the sun is actually more powerful. The results of exposure during the rains is generally, however, more permanently injurious, though frequently no indications of its deleterious effects are perceptible till the excitement has passed away.

During the evening of the 1st of June several natives called and informed me that the 5th Native Infantry were disposing of all their personal property in the city for anything it would realize and much below its intrinsic value, converting, in fact, all they possessed into cash. The inference naturally drawn by these residents of the city, that the 5th had made up their minds, was clearly a correct one. The time and complexion of the outbreak was now the only question. As neither the 29th nor the 4th Lancers were showing any equally undisguised indications of following suit, we hoped for the best. Captain G——n, distrusting, nevertheless trusted his own men, to whom he was much attached; it was vain for the rest to act otherwise. In the prevention of an outbreak we were helpless, and constant anxiety had induced an almost inconceivable callousness; our position had frequently been in appearance more imminently threatening.

A native gentleman, who was fond of shooting, and in quieter times had sometimes accompanied me when in the vicinity of jungles, and leisure was found for short excursions, had then become as intimate with me as it is prudent in a civil officer in India to permit with the ever-crafty Hindustani. He was of that stamp of native rarely to be found in northern India, amongst the generally contemptibly effeminate wealthier classes; he was manly, loved manly sports, and as a natural result was neither gifted with that cringing flattery nor insolent arrogance, rather, as it may be termed, sickly impudence, extremes everywhere manifested by this class in the North-West, and which it seems, as a rule, impossible for them to avoid. He, in fact, understood his position, and how to meet you as a gentleman, and the notorious Nana's elder brother was another of the few exceptions I have met with. This native gentleman's name was Oosmân Khân, a resident of Belaspore, distant some fifteen miles from the town of Saharunpore. From the commencement of the mutiny, he constantly visited me, whenever I was in the station or encamped anywhere within reach of Belaspore. There was a mutual kindliness of feeling between us, and I was glad to see him. At first, before perceiving that the mutiny was actually a rebellion, in which he might improve his position, his visits did, I think, originate honestly, and his advice was certainly good. Day after day did he reiterate that the only policy which could now in our position possibly succeed was severity in the extreme; that death must now become the only punishment for the slightest opposition, and that any deviation from this course would insure the loss of the district. But when the storm was closing thicker round us, I noticed that he visited me, still unchanged in manner, in company with Deedar Singh, the head of the Bunjarahs. Deedar Singh, though a man powerful amongst his clan, was, in many respects, but a simple-minded Bunjarah, or cow-herd, totally unable to cope with Oosmân Khân. Mahomedans and Bunjarahs* are by nature deadly enemies, and it was easy to perceive that the wily old Mahomedan, whatever his personal attachments might be, was playing a deep game; he wished to enlist on his side the powerful clan of Bunjarahs, and Deedar Singh was evidently falling into his meshes. These two men together could, if necessary, muster the whole population of the northern portion of the district, which, though not numerous, were hardy, well armed, and accustomed to use their arms in killing game and wild animals.

When to all it appeared very doubtful if we could hold out much longer, Oosmân Khân pressed me to take shelter in his ghurie, or fort, if obliged to fly. The offer was, I think, kindly meant, and he might,

* Bunjarahs adore the cow; and this tribe of them wander with their extensive herds over the waste lands and jungles on the north and north-east of the Saharunpore district. Often have I noticed when in the jungles, and anxious to procure a bullock, as a bait for a tiger, that their influence rendered it impossible for me to do so, unless the animal was sent for from a considerable distance; the foolish creatures not possessing the foresight to observe that the very tiger that might be killed was every second night carrying off some of their pet cattle, while even the bullock required would probably not be killed.

in conjunction with Deedar Singh, also a friend of mine, have protected me if necessary; but the feelings of a conquering race overcame even the kindest offers of the conquered when reverses have put the former on their metal, and Oosmân Khân was distinctly informed that never would an Englishman request shelter from a native. "No wonder," was the reply, "there has been so much treachery;" yet, so true was he to the Hindustani character, I could never detect any change in this man's behaviour to me, and frequently did he repeat the offer.

When Delhi had fallen, and no doubt remained in the native mind which side would be victorious, Oosmân Khân and Deedar Singh ceased to be seen together; the natural animosities of a hostile race and creed were left to play in their full vigour, now that Oosmân Khân's interest to be civil had ceased, while his dupe, Deedar Singh, seemed to me almost ashamed of the intimacy he had permitted the former to establish with him.

On the 2nd of June, the disaffected of the 5th Native Infantry gradually worked themselves up to the necessary state of excitement. Though the course the mutineers intended to adopt had been clearly defined, the knowing ones were aware that, with well-timed excitement, many of the loyally disposed might join. Most of us distrusted every man in the regiment, notwithstanding Captain G——n's confidence in his men, for all previous knowledge of sepoys had invariably proved valueless. Yet there were actually two violently antagonistic parties in this regiment, and the loyal were as strong and determined as the mutineers. Had we been able to oppose to them Europeans, and thus excited the deep race jealousies of the time, all to a man would probably have turned against us; as it was, the wild native impulses, with no opposition to develop them, were subdued by time for practical reflection.

The detachment of the 5th Native Infantry happened to be temporarily encamped in one corner of the grounds belonging to the house in which most of us were living, and the house was within easy musket range of their camp. An order to march early the following morning in the direction of Umballah was issued to the 5th Native Infantry, about 5 P.M. on the 2nd of June. This, they at once argued, would place them in the power of Europeans, and Captain G——n was informed that it was their intention to disobey the order. This pointed disaffection was too much even for Captain G——n, who now came over to where those in the bath-house were assembled. The case was discussed, when Captain W——d suggested that, as all did not seem unanimous in the wish to disobey orders, those who had made up their minds not to march had better be informed that their services were not required. Captain G——n disapproved; he still clung to the hope of keeping his men to their duty. As Captain

W——d's suggestion was, however, clearly the best course, he assumed his position as senior officer then in the station, and ordered the suggestion to be carried out. He himself, with a civilian, then accompanied Captain G——n to the encampment. The men were called together. It was clearly explained to them, that all who desired to continue no longer in the government service would be paid up, and receive their discharge in due form. A list of the men was then produced and read out, and instructions given that, on each name being called, the man, if he wished to remain in the service, was to join the officers; if not, he was to fall back. Those first on the list came forward, but, one by one, they began to fall back, till the mutineers gained strength and courage enough to jeer at all those who joined their officers. It was remarked, at the time, that the mutineers so fell back as to be near the spot where the arms were piled, and that this portion of the drama passed off quietly must be attributed entirely to the extraordinary influence possessed by Captain G——n over his men. Captain G——n and the civilian now retired into a tent close at hand, waiting for the money which had been sent for from the civil treasury to meet the legitimate demands of those supposed to be retiring from the service, and where the details of the arrangement could be carried out; while one of the party, Captain W——d, continued with the men.

Those in the tent shortly sent a man to summon the first on the list, to receive his arrears and discharge. This man, leading all the disaffected, called out that their arms must accompany them: these they at once seized, and began loading. Captain W——d now ordered the well-affected to load also, which they did; but they pressed him to be off to his own men, the 4th Lancers, declaring their inability to protect him. Seeing the game was up, Captain W——d made for his own troopers, who were encamped a short distance beyond the compound boundary in the regular encamping ground. The mutineers anticipated him; firing commenced, and certain of them closed in between him and the cavalry, which necessitated a move towards the house in front of which most of us were seated.

"Wolf" had so often been the cry, that carelessness had gradually supervened and modified our usual precautions. Most of our small party of Europeans, excepting those who had been in the bath-house, were not assembled at our rallying point when the plot actually developed itself. I myself had driven out towards the native city, accompanied by a friend, with the object of taking a hurried view of the state of things in that direction. True, we had added a couple of rifles to our ordinary armament of pistols; but the usual order for saddled horses had not been issued by me, and two others were dependent on my horses, which were kept, as usual, in their own stables. Most of our party, I think, kept their horses at the rendezvous ; but, being ill and dead beat with exposure, I preferred living alone, where quiet was a possibility, and my arrangements were shaped accordingly. A second party of three had also gone out driving in a dog-cart in another direction, but totally unarmed, whilst our officiating artilleryman was visiting his house, though not far off.

My friend and myself had hardly dismounted and seated ourselves in front of the rendezvous house, when the first shot at Captain W——d was fired. The subsequent rapid firing, in our direction too, put us on our metal. As the others there seated ran in for their arms, our artilleryman galloped up. Our guns consisted of one three-quarter and one half pounder, probably more dangerous to friends than foes. They had been sent to us by the Ranee of Landhoura, and were poor specimens of bad native guns, not less than a hundred years old; however, they answered our purpose. The name of such a possession was something, and all loyal natives were in confidence informed that grape and canister had been made up for the said guns. The best of the two was rapidly loaded with canister and wheeled out to the edge of the balustrade facing the sepoys, who were within rifle-shot, but we did not return their salute, agreeing to reserve our fire till every shot would tell. In a short time we saw Captain W——d coming towards us with sepoys in pursuit, and could not but come to the conclusion that the 4th Lancers had also joined in the mutiny. It was now growing dusk, which, with the dust and utter confusion, added much to the indistinctness of passing events. We could, however, make out that the majority of the men before us were at this instant turning from the direction of the house, and going towards the Meeruth road. None of us doubted that the whole of the 5th at least had mutinied, and wondered that they did not come to close quarters. The internal dissension partly caused this, though they had not much to fear from the loyal, but they were true to their race as sepoys.* Daring to a degree when the

* The combination of cowardice and pluck amongst Hindustanis is still to me an incomprehensible enigma; for I have known and seen acts performed by them in contests with wild animals that few Englishmen would attempt; nor can such an ordeal be scorned, as these contests are eminently conducive to the formation of that boldness, combined with cool, active presence of mind in emergencies, which are alone formidable in the character of a nation. The instances of these unequal contests are numerous, and all who have lived much in the vicinity of Indian forests are well acquainted with such cases. To relate only a single example:—When I was once encamped in the neighbourhood of Islâmnugur, one of the larger species of leopard seized and carried off a Rajpoot, ploughing his field near my tents. Two of the man's relations, armed with swords alone, at once gave chase, overtook the leopard, and actually cut him down in fair open fight. They recovered the body of their relative at the expense of some slight wounds, and sent the leopard's skin to me. Few Europeans thus armed would face the leopard or tiger; a feat which is common enough in these jungle tracts, and the race that can produce men possessing the nerve capable of achieving these actions must not be too much despised in consequence of their cowardice during the late revolt, as increase of intelligence may yet enable them to direct aright the strength they doubtless possess.

minimum of danger was to be encountered, they would not face a discharge of the dreaded grape and a few rifles. The firing having ceased, to us as yet unaccountably, we were joined from another direction by the two who had been in the tent; we expected that they might be able to enlighten us, but they seemed even more ignorant than ourselves of the actual position of affairs, for, shortly after arriving, they pressed a few men of the 29th, then on guard at a small house in the compound, to attack the 5th. This they refused to do, pleading the necessity of guarding the post assigned to them. There was a small supply of treasure in the house, so that the grounds of their refusal were legitimate, had we not ourselves posted them there, and they were bound to obey the senior officer present. Their conduct we naturally looked on with suspicion; they might attack us in rear, but their refusal to act was most fortunate. The only men they could then have attacked were the faithful, through whose fidelity, though apparently unaware of it, the tenants of the tent were then in existence. The mutineers should, however, receive the credit due to them of not firing in the direction even of their favourite officers' tent. After much hesitation, some of the party went up to the faithful of the 5th. It then appeared that not only had the sepoys assembled there not remained passive spectators, but had actually shot down one of the mutineers, when attempting to intercept Captain

W——d. This was the first case of the kind we had even heard of.

It was mentioned above that one party went out unarmed in a dog-cart and happened to be returning by the very road the mutineers had taken. The constant heavy discharge of fire-arms was so common in the city and neighbourhood in those days that the firing had not attracted the attention of this party as at all peculiar. The sepoys they noticed ahead of them, and thought little of it. Fortunately their horse at this juncture stumbled and fell, and all were then thrown out of the dog-cart. The mutineers, brimfull of suspicion, at once assumed that this accident must be a knowing device for escape, and calling out "Mar! mar!" began firing. Distance, dusk, and their heels saved the officers' lives. The evident intention of the sepoys was to let the officers drive into the midst of them, and when within ten yards the game would have been safe enough. Had their guilty suspicions not been aroused, and their firing commenced as described, the officers would probably have walked through this body of sepoys on foot, as they had no reason to suspect these men in particular. Their escape was altogether providential.

The squall cleared off just before it became very dark, when a patrol of the 4th Lancers was sent in pursuit of the mutineers. Naturally, they could not be found. The demonstration was politic, while darkness formed a plausible excuse for want of success—in itself a success. On reviewing our position, we found that the 29th had all remained staunch at their post over the civil treasury, about half a mile distant. They had no idea of sharing the treasure with the 5th Native Infantry; it was all their own legitimate property by the established usages of the revolt, and circumstances might yet enable them to become sole proprietors. The 4th Lancers too, with the exception of a few deserters, were still at work, so we could now begin again, and hope for the best, till the next cause of excitement should spring up. The mutineers, both of the 4th and 5th, had left without the arrears of pay due to them, and the bag, with the money intended for them, was left untouched by any one.

On this evening I noticed that even the really loyal men were excited to a pitch that only religious fanaticism could account for, which was, doubtless, the motive force brought to bear upon the uninitiated. Never had I seen natives thus peculiarly excited, except in the case of the 29th at the encamping ground at Kheree previously referred to. It seemed a greater effort to resist the demon of mutiny than to obey his inspirations; the effort had overstrained their minds; they could not comprehend their position; some were talking wildly, others seized violently the arms of Europeans, and declared that no harm should happen to us, at any rate whilst *they* were alive. They were, for the time, sincere, though, in a few weeks, many of these too were engulphed in the irresistible stream.*

More than ordinary good conduct and fidelity on the part of two of my servants was evinced during this mutiny of the 5th Native Infantry. When the fire was thickest, we saw a man hurriedly leading a horse close in front of the line of sepoys. My astonishment was considerable on recognizing that the man was my Mahomedan groom, Hussan Khâñ, with one of my horses. He did not get very far, however, before the animal, excited by the firing, knocked him down, broke away, and galloped off. The groom was lost sight of, but a moment or two after, another servant, Kukundoo, a half-caste, between an Oude Rajpoot and a Passee,† made his appearance on my small Burmah pony; he brought two more guns and a

* For another account of this mutiny, *vide* Appendix.

† The Passees, called in some parts Pausees, are a race of low-caste Hindoos, chiefly found in Oude and the jungle tracts bordering on that province. They are robbers and thieves by profession, while all are keen and skilful sportsmen. The poorest amongst them, prior to the revolt, generally possessed an old rusty gun or matchlock, which they had almost universally adopted as more useful than their bows and arrows, with which they had formerly the reputation of being expert marksmen. This class being so well armed, and naturally of a lawless disposition, became very troublesome during the late revolt to both friends and foes. The men of property in Oude generally pay the Passees a species of black mail, by employing members of the clan as watchmen, in which capacity they are generally faithful, and the rest of the clan hold sacred the property of a man engaging one of their number.

sword, and was loaded with bags of ammunition. I picked up this man some years before as a boy—rather a ragamuffin, too—at Cawnpore, where he was a camp follower of the 74th Native Infantry. He always accompanied me on my shooting expeditions, and he had become a dead shot, even at snipe, an accomplishment rarely acquired by a native. At such a moment he was a valuable addition to our small force, for all trusted him. He said he had come to accompany me if flight was necessary; but, as my horse had escaped, he handed the pony, extra guns, and ammunition over to me, and ran off for another steed. My plucky Mahomedan groom had, however, anticipated him. Disappointed in his first bold effort, he at once returned to my house, quickly saddled another horse, and managed to bring it to me by a more circuitous track. I certainly never expected the Mahomedan to act thus. This man was also a native of Oude. After the fall of Delhi, when my duties led me down country with the columns then reoccupying the Ganges-Jumna Doab, this man found himself not far from his home, situated near the left bank of the Ganges. He was naturally extremely anxious to visit his native village, to ascertain the situation of his family and what had been the effect of the revolt on those dearest to him. As he resembled a sepoy, and knowing that his appearance would be against him, I refused to sanction this leave, and he marched about the country with me a few months longer; but again nearing his home, I was weak enough to grant the leave so anxiously solicited, though only for a term within which I knew that that portion of the country would not be reoccupied. He never returned; and, after much inquiry, some of my other servants brought information that the poor fellow had been mistaken for a sepoy, and killed during a sudden attack made on his village, in consequence of parties from that neighbourhood plundering or threatening the right bank of the Ganges. Though these two servants so unexpectedly behaved well, the head native amongst my servants never made his appearance. Being a resident of Oude, and belonging to the same village as many of the sepoys, this head servant might easily have furnished me with valuable information, if so inclined, but I never could get anything out of him, though I afterwards ascertained that he had a very good idea of the plans of the mutineers, as it was the interest of the sepoys to be on good terms with him, for the sake of such information as Hindustani servants amongst Hindustanis are invariably supposed to possess, he being supplied with scraps of intelligence in return.

CHAPTER V.

Arrival of the Nusseeree Battalion at Saharunpore—Disgraceful panic at Simla—The position of the Europeans at Simla—Probability that the Nusseerees might mutiny—Attack on rebels summoned by the 29th Native Infantry—Intentions of the 29th Native Infantry frustrated by the arrival of the Goorkhas—Ride over to Roorkie with horse police—Peculiar importance of the revenue—Chances of turning our own establishments against us—Present and future of Roorkie—The Khâdir lands of the Ganges—Devoted gallantry of two officers at Roorkie—Mutiny of the sappers—Position of the Europeans at Roorkie—Short-sighted policy of the officer in command, and its results—Importance of the removal of ladies and children to places of safety in the event of an outbreak—Their presence paralyses the action of the men—The presence of ladies and children the cause of the Futtehgurh massacre—Realization of the revenue at Roorkie—Jwalla Pershad, the tuhseeldar of Roorkie—His opinions on the revolt—Our legislation—Its effect both on the higher and lower orders—Litigation encouraged by the power of appeal — Importance of employing native agency in official positions in India—Extension of official European agency impolitic—Non-official Europeans an advantage to the country.

The Nusseeree Battalion, 300 strong, sent to us by the Punjaub authorities, arrived at Saharunpore on the morning of the 3rd of June. We all rejoiced in this exchange of Hindustanis for Goorkha troops; but the Nusseerees brought with them the cholera, a less welcome guest. This regiment had been the origin of one of the worst panics that ever disgraced the name of Englishman. The Redan and the 14th Dragoons at Chilleanwallah have given rise to the impression that private soldiers alone are the class subject to panics; but at Simla there were none. The Nusseerees had shown a decidedly mutinous spirit at Jutob, when ordered to march without leaving the usual guard of their own men over their women, a point on which they are extremely jealous. Jutob is some four or five miles from Simla, and separated from it by defensible ravines. At the latter place the English residents, amongst whom there must have been, including officers, civilians, and shopkeepers, from 150 to 200 men, instead of uniting and holding their own, which, for the protection of the ladies and children, was absolutely necessary, actually fled, and scattered in all directions. The chief military and civil authorities residing in the place took the lead in this disgraceful evasion, and, what is hardly credible, they left the ladies and children, whose husbands and fathers were fighting in the plains, to take care of themselves. Had actual mutiny occurred at Jutob, there were few places in India, except Meeruth, where the approximation to equality in the respective numbers of the English and the mutineers would have been so favourable to the former; and yet it was only here where the disgrace of unnecessary flight tarnished the English name.

There were some, however, inspired with the spirit elsewhere exhibited during this revolt. Lord W. H——, the deputy commissioner of Simla, and the officers of the Nusseerees, in spite of the defection of the other Europeans, remained at their posts, where it eventually turned out the danger had been exaggerated. The Simla *bolters* being men in authority, and only too anxious to cover their own disgraceful conduct, on arriving in Umballah, spread the most wild and exaggerated reports regarding the conduct of the Nusseerees; so that their original destination, Delhi, was changed; and they were, most fortunately for the Saharunpore district, sent to test their loyalty on us. On the advent, then, of a regiment possessing so unpleasant a notoriety, we could not but now and then reflect that we were perhaps booked for a second edition of the 5th Native Infantry business; though, somehow, most of us from the first, in reality, placed considerable confidence in the new arrivals. The very day after they came, we took them out to attack a body of rebels assembled some five miles distance from the station, who had been emboldened by the previous day's mutiny to come to close quarters. Long afterwards, I ascertained that the 29th Native Infantry, having by the mutiny of the previous day got rid of the 5th, who might have disputed the possession of the treasure with them, had invited these rebellious villagers to attack us and plunder the station, while they were comfortably walking off with the treasure under their charge. The plans of both parties were consequently frustrated by the unexpected arrival of the Nusseerees, while the discomfited rebels dispersed themselves amongst ravines on our advance with the Goorkhas, and not a shot was fired; though, as usual, our gallant horse police, ever foremost in the absence of danger, managed to inflict some severe gashes on a few unresisting villagers; but such irregularities it was now impossible to restrain.

As in some portions of the district between Saharunpore and Roorkie there had been considerable gatherings, attended with outrages, and no revenue had been received, I rode over on the morning of the 5th of June to the latter place, some twenty-five miles distant, accompanied by a few native horsemen. Revenue was now to us of more vital importance than in the other one or two districts in the North-West, where English authority was partially maintained by the presence of European bayonets. In ordinary times, the Saharunpore district always received assistance in meeting its heavy disbursements. Left to our own resources, without Europeans to enforce submission, we had large native establishments which must either be maintained or they would assuredly turn against us. Paid from our treasury were the head-quarters of the Canal Department of the North-West Provinces, with its workshops and civil engineering college at Roorkie; the canal police and workmen for both the Ganges and Eastern Jumna canals; an extensive remounting stud and botanical gardens, independently of our own police and revenue establishments, which had been greatly enlarged. The natives engaged in these various establishments, with their relatives and dependants, scattered all over the district, would continue loyal so long only as regular pay was forthcoming; it therefore became impolitic to dismiss even those whose services were not required, as their loyalty formed an interested bulwark against the progress of revolt. Amongst the majority of natives, pay regularly met will induce submission to serious shortcomings and actual grievances. Money was, therefore, necessary, and the only possible means of obtaining it was by the collection of the revenue. Accompanied by a few mounted police, to further my views, as I expected no fighting, Roorkie for a few days became the centre of my movements.

Roorkie is situated on the right bank of the Solani, at the point where the noble aqueduct of the Ganges Canal spans that river. On elevated ground overlooking an extensive tract, encircled to the north by the snowy ranges of the Himalayas, and bounded to the west by the Ganges Canal, here of the dimensions of a river, the position of Roorkie is, in many respects, well chosen. It is at present in a very retired and thinly-peopled portion of the district, bordering on the extensive Khâdir* jungle of the Ganges; but this Khâdir is amongst the richest and most valuable land in the district, which is also the case with some of the jungle tract to the north; consequently, when these waste lands are peopled and cultivated, Roorkie will assume greater importance. Prior to the mutiny of the sappers at Roorkie, this place had been the scene of one of those innumerable instances of devotion in the discharge of their duty so conspicuous among Englishmen throughout this revolt.

Six companies of the sappers, who had been sent from Roorkie to Meeruth, immediately on the outbreak had mutinied at the latter place, and killed their commanding officer, Captain E. Frazer. Two companies of this regiment had been retained in the cantonments at Roorkie, and, on receiving the news of the mutiny of their corps at Meeruth, the men at Roorkie became very excited. At extreme personal risk, Captain D——d and Lieutenant B——m, neither then belonging to the regiment, proposed to live and sleep in the quarter guard with the men to quiet their suspicions. This act of devotion continued till the 18th of May, when, at the earnest request of certain of the native officers and men, the officers left the lines during that night; and early the following morning, after a slight encounter amongst themselves, the sappers

* Low alluvial lands, formed by most of the large Indian rivers.

left the place in the direction of the Khâdir of the Ganges, committing no injury beyond ill-treating a few of the fifty amongst them who remained loyal. Thus terminated almost all immediate anxiety for the safety of the ladies and children in Roorkie.

On my arrival at Roorkie, I found that the Europeans had fortified the workshops by forming entrenchments, and had mounted some rather good old Seikh guns captured in the Punjaub campaign, of which they were the happy possessors, and which excited in my breast no inconsiderable amount of envy. All the ladies and children were living in the workshops, while the men kept regular guards, and patrolled the immediate neighbourhood.

Either not comprehending the nature of the revolt, or trusting to the quietness of the position, the ladies and the children at Roorkie had not been removed to the hills when this was possible. Now the roads were closed to such travellers as were unable to defend themselves. This garrison was, for the time, safe; but consulting their own safety alone in such a crisis became not only a selfish, but also a short-sighted policy. In a station with an intelligent and valuable, though small body of Europeans, all efforts, with the helpless charge in the workshops, were now necessarily confined to the immediate neighbourhood of Roorkie. The protection of the ladies and children became the paramount object, preventing the Europeans in Roorkie from adding to the strength of the district by crushing rebellion at a distance; and had the dangerous portions of this district not been successfully restrained by others, who counted their Europeans by units, not by tens, the whole force of the rebellion would have converged on this spot, hampered with women and children.

As, for many reasons, it seems indispensable that European ladies and women should be encouraged to accompany their husbands or relations in India, there should be handed over to civilians in outlying districts, or officers commanding outposts or stations, where no European troops are located, a carefully drawn-up set of instructions as to how the ladies and children are to be disposed of, in the event of the country becoming disturbed, otherwise the English nation will again witness an exaggerated form of the horrors of the past. The ladies and children being at once removed to places of safety, the men are free to act as becomes Englishmen, or can retreat in comparative safety, which would be impossible when hampered with so helpless a charge, whose presence might eventually prove fatal to all. Thus, at Futtehgurh, had the ladies and children, while the roads were open—which they were for a considerable time after the Meeruth outbreak—been removed to Agra, only some eighty miles distant, the gentlemen could, when they saw that further efforts to maintain order were useless, have mounted their horses and cantered into that place, as the 10th Native Infantry, stationed at Futtehgurh, proved that they would never have injured them. As it was, when the revolt thickened, the unfortunate residents of Futtehgurh, hampered with women and children, dared not move across a rebel tract of no great extent, and we know the result of the trip down the river, or subsequent tenure of the fort of Futtehgurh. On this subject, then, distinct orders should be given to those in charge of outposts, who, on so vital a point, should not have free scope to indulge the whim of the moment. All idea of rendering natives more loyal by a semblance of confidence, so frequently tried during this revolt, when the line of action originating therefrom is actually weakening one's own hands, is but a cruelly suicidal policy, for Hindustanis are quite sharp enough to see through it at once, and chuckle over our weak credulity, which is placing us hopelessly in their power.

From the 5th of June I remained a few days in the neighbourhood of Roorkie, visiting many of the larger villages or towns within range. Those who considered they had implicated themselves in rebellion, generally abandoned their homes on my approach, but no resistance was offered; my only object was to intimidate,* the straightest road to a native's heart, and these visits had the desired effect.

* An old Hindustani proverb has it, "Kick a man first, and then speak to him;" or, impress him with your power and he will be civil. The Hindustani probably understands the character of his own race.

The revenue came in, and excused my returning to the welcome shelter of a house. The heat was intense, and constant hard riding in a June sun, with little rest since the outbreak, had left its traces. Excitement, however, is for the time a powerful and providential tonic.

At Roorkie, the chief revenue and police officer of the pergunnah (or county) was a Cashmere Brahmun, named Jwalla Pershad: he spoke and wrote English fluently; was, in common with all the Brahmuns, particularly those from Cashmere, clever and intelligent; and, being a foreigner, the sincerity of his avowed impressions regarding the revolt was probably less questionable. On inquiring from this man how it was that the higher classes amongst the natives, who were generally well informed, had been induced to join in a revolt originating ostensibly in a supposed loss of caste, Jwalla Pershad remarked that the higher classes had hated the English ever since they had been deprived of their former power over the lower orders. Another important reason was named. They asserted that when we first entered India we courted their society, and through their influence conquered the country, which we could not have accomplished with native troops unsupported by the good-will of their superiors; that now, having subdued the whole country, so far from courting their society, we had ceased to be even civil to them, while subverting their ancestral rights in the soil and its cultivators formerly their virtual slaves. They felt, in fact, that we were exactly in the position of the man in the fable, who assisted the horse to catch his enemy. Nor is it possible to deny the truth of much of this, which chiefly arises from a confused accumulation of good intentions on our part. A country hardly emerging from barbarism, we trammel with complex laws and regulations adapted to one in an advanced stage of civilization; we endeavour to make the infant run before it can walk, which rough treatment it naturally resents, while our extreme kindness is rewarded by the distrust of the more ignorant portion of the population and the hatred of the better informed.

It is far from my intention to advocate any but a progressive policy in India; but there are distinct methods of progress, and I feel that we have not been sufficiently alive to the importance of making material progress precede legislation for a people thus circumstanced. In our earlier possessions, our policy, while we repressed violence, was to leave everything as much as possible as we found it; our rule thus became popular, and enabled us to advance to further conquests. The civil officer in those days merely exercised a general, careless supervision, his native subordinates doubtless accomplishing enough iniquity; but it was carried out in accordance with native ideas; even the poorer classes liked it, while the rich had more consideration shown to them, and were happy. With less work to engage his time, the civil officer had more leisure to devote to interviews with native gentlemen. These were free to come at all times, and enter into long palavers with the head of the district, than which nothing more delights them, as they thus acquire greater consideration amongst their own retainers, and John Bull even may understand how to sympathise with this feeling. In our days, on the contrary, the meshes of the legislative net have yearly been drawn smaller, till they at last circumvent every imaginable riggling little fish that had far better have been allowed to escape from the confounding talons of that harpy called appeal, which renders the action of our courts utterly incomprehensible to all but the city sharpers or highly respectable pleaders in Sudder Adauluts. With the increase of legislation, the official returns, too, required from district officers, who are the servants of many masters, being most perplexingly multiplied, with no proportionate addition to the subordinate staff of the district, the work at times, and that, too, in a tropical climate, is heavier almost than anything known even in the English metropolis. Excepting when at his meals, the civilian has often no moment of the day to himself; and, after twenty-five years of this slavery in India, it is hardly to be wondered at that he is frequently totally worn out.

One consequence of this increasing work is, that

civilians generally have no time to engage in the interesting conversations so loved by native gentlemen. The respectable old landholder or city capitalist considers it a duty to pay his respects now and then to the head of the district; but how is this achieved? After being detained in an ante-room perhaps half an hour or more, he is ushered into the presence; both parties bow politely; half-a-dozen words are exchanged; another bow and the conversation must end, or the civil officer's work falls into arrears. Men entitled to consideration in the district justly complain, but the remedy lies not in the civil officer's power.

Litigation in our courts, instead of being encouraged by the power of appeal, should and could be easily diminished to the mutual benefit of both governors and governed. All legislation that increases the number of cases brought under the direct cognizance of Europeans, as steadily increases the native hatred of the foreign race. Govern kindly and well by all means, but do not let an Englishman appear in the transaction at all, if possible. There is a universal cry amongst the European press in India for an increase of the European agency in the minor civil appointments, which the natives do doubtless constantly abuse. But it would be impossible to obtain respectable Europeans to accept those appointments on anything like the present allowances; and, even were those allowances doubled, the experiment would be a dangerous one. It may be an unpalatable assertion, but it is, nevertheless, not far from the mark, that ill-paid Europeans in India, if their position affords facilities for it, do generally, though the exceptions may be numerous, after a few years' experience, combine with all the native love of intrigue and bribery that indomitable English pluck which eventually carries them far beyond the Hindustani, and renders them, both to the pecuniary interests and reputation of the Government, infinitely more dangerous. This refers to very minor appointments, such as road superintendentships, &c.; but, expand the experiment, and the result would simply be dishonour to the English name, loss of revenue to Government, and downright hatred of the conquering race. If the discredit of bribery is to be attached to any one, let the natives be able to accuse their own race alone, and look up as heretofore to the Europeans possessing power in their districts as unapproachable by such influences. Encourage Europeans, by all means, to enter the country as indigo planters, merchants, or other occupations independent of the Government, and the native will always meet them half way; but it is our policy to let the natives feel as much as possible that they are governed by natives, and that the European is present in the district merely to prevent the abuse of power by his own countrymen. The native will thus lose sight of the constant presence of official members of the conquering race at times, even with the best intentions, committing injustice through the incessant perjury of all litigants. I have constantly seen an injured man with a case, if truthfully stated, as clear as daylight, under the impression that he was strengthening his position, so utterly confuse its important features by the introduction of false evidence, that it eventually became a matter of great doubt what were the real facts of the case, and whether your own conclusion was correct. However, the less natives are governed directly by Europeans, the less trouble will they give, and the more happy and contented will they become. The civil administration of the country will thus alone maintain a certain degree of popularity; for Hindustanis, like men of other nations, take kindly the abuses committed by their own race, while wildly exaggerating those of Europeans.

CHAPTER VI.

Return to Saharunpore—Gloomy nature of the news from all quarters—Jullunder mutineers appear on the banks of the Jumna—March of the first party through the Saharunpore district—The second division—Long marches of the rebels—Attempt to intercept them at Khera—Their retreat—Sepoys absent on furlough during the hot season—An important advantage to the British cause—Result of the march of mutineers through the district—Requisition made by the tuhseeldar of Nookur—My march to assist him—First impressions on being joined by the Rajah of Putteealah's body guard—Advance with the cavalry—Approach Nookur—Find the city in flames—Difficulty in procuring information—Active energy of the rebels—Visit the ruins of the Government offices—Pursuit of the rebels at daybreak—Hindustani objection to engaging in enterprises during the night—Our party fired at by villagers—We attack the place—Further advance—A party intercepted—Women employed on these expeditions—Our return to Nookur—Removal of our camp—The whole country rises to attack us—Impossibility of retreat without sacrificing the infantry—Remove to a brick-kiln—Measures of defence—Horsemen despatched for reinforcements—The night passed on the brick-kiln—Arrival of Fureed Bux with his detachment of the 15th Irregulars—Approach of reinforcements in the morning.

On returning to Saharunpore, after the expedition mentioned in the preceding chapter, I found our small party in much the same situation as when I left. They were still living in one house, though the conduct of the Nusseerees had been such as to inspire much confidence. Rest was indispensable to myself while there was a chance of it, but the discomfort of a crowded house precluded this; my own, though I should there be alone, was consequently preferable to one totally exhausted both in mind and body. Without desiring to dismiss the usual Hindustani guard at my house, who had shown no indications of disaffection, it must be confessed that I at times felt a little too much at their mercy. This protracted feeling of uncertainty had now, however, become almost a second nature; while the tidings of disaster from all quarters arriving in a confused form, often totally incorrect, and always long after date, only rendered our horizon daily darker and more gloomy. Massacre on massacre, but the storm seemed only to be gathering its strength; the worst had not yet come; twenty-four hours' rest, and I longed again for activity; the natives must feel that they were dealing with Englishmen.

Hardly had the wish arisen than the Jullunder mutineers made their appearance on the banks of the Jumna. They crossed on rafts, but divided into two parties, to enable this to be carried into effect more rapidly. The first party, some 200 strong, passed through the district so rapidly in the Delhi direction, that all plans and calculations were frustrated. Saharunpore, we concluded, they certainly intended to attack, and could not at the time assign any other reason for their move across the Jumna,

Delhi being on the right bank of that river. Their first march from Rajpore was thirty-five miles, and their second equally long; but we were not aware that we were dealing with men thoroughly frightened. Shortly after this, the second party, from 300 to 400 strong, marched down with even more rapid strides. The experience of the first party's movements now assisted us. After much discussion regarding the direction we should take, with 150 of the Nusseerees and some of the 15th Irregular Cavalry, we very nearly intercepted the mutineers at a place called Khera, some eighteen to twenty miles south-west of Saharunpore; but they were here before us, after a march of forty-six miles without a halt. On these marches, the sepoys invariably seized all horses, elephants, and camels they could put their hands on, and it was consequently impossible for ordinary infantry to come up with them.

On approaching Khera, the enemy's cavalry showed themselves in front of some groves of mangoe trees, which were surrounded with a belt of brushwood, a quarter of a mile deep. We had, therefore, to advance very cautiously, the enemy's cavalry gradually retreating. By the time we had passed the first set of groves and reached the village, the cavalry galloped off, and we found that the infantry had abandoned the neighbourhood some time. The cavalry were left merely to deceive us and retard our advance, thereby enabling the infantry to get a good start, which being successfully accomplished, they vanished. The mutineers had entered an extensive jungle to the south of the village, and it was now becoming dark. I had often shot in this jungle, and knew the hopelessness and danger of pursuit during the night, so we quietly lay down in an open space before the village until the morning, the enemy having in the meantime made another long march. I have often thanked my stars we had no fight that evening. The rebels were vastly superior to us in every respect; the Nusseerees had not recovered from their Simla notoriety, and in the fight the 15th Irregulars would probably have gone over to the enemy, attacking us in rear or flank. The 15th Irregulars had been originally raised in the Saharunpore district, and these men were those absent on leave from their regiment when the revolt commenced. It was the custom in the Company's army to grant a very considerable portion of the men in each native regiment four or six months' furlough during the hot season, when parades were not so numerous. Subsequent investigations proved to me that the majority of these men on furlough were actively engaged against the Government; still, in consequence of being scattered all over the country, and unable generally to join their own particular regiments, they were actually of little value to the rebels. The mutiny commencing as it did, early in the hot season, when so many men were absent on furlough, the effective strength of each regiment was very materially reduced; and in so large an army as that of Bengal, this was by no means an inconsiderable advantage to the British cause.

These 15th, with a few men belonging to other irregular cavalry regiments, being armed, for the arms and horses of irregulars are their own property, had just been summoned from their homes in a rebellious portion of the district through our police, and knew none of the Europeans. The whole thing was an experiment, which none but men in our position would have ventured to adopt. There was no officer to take charge of the 15th in the field, while we knew that their regiment had mutinied, killing its commanding officer at Sultanpore; and, though professing horror of the deed, they were Hindustanis and Mahomedans.

Our miserable position had doubtless been already sufficiently exaggerated, when the passage of the mutinous troops through the western portion of the district, and unchecked, rapidly convinced a wavering and ignorant population that our power was really on the decline; and that now, if ever, was there a chance for a fling at anarchy. The district was actually looking quieter than usual, when an urgent requisition for assistance appeared from a tuhseeldar, or head native revenue and police officer of a pergunnah or county. He anticipated a serious attack on the government Tuhseelee and Thanah* at Nookur. Allowing, however, for the usual exaggeration of natives, the affair did not look to me very serious; so I started with but a few men for Nookur. Besides three Europeans of our Saharunpore party who volunteered to accompany me, my force consisted of thirty of the Nusseerees and forty Seikh horse of the Rajah of Putteealah's body guard. The latter had just been sent over by the Punjaub authorities, and they proved a useful body of men.

On the 20th of June, on as fiery an afternoon as this season of the year in the North-West Provinces usually produces, I left the station of Saharunpore, accompanied by these Nusseerees and Seikhs, with both of whom I was now destined to spend many a weary night's march, or engage in doubtful expeditions. The Goorkhas had been supplied with bullock carts by Captain M——l, the officer in charge of the stud, so as to save their making a long march on foot, and thus render them effective, if fighting was destined to be the order of the day on arriving at our destination. In consequence of the state of the cross roads, however, we progressed but slowly; and as there might be really more in the tuhseeldar's report than I was quite

* Tuhseelee, the revenue office and treasury of a pergunnah, or county, in which the tuhseeldar transacts his duties. Thanah, the head-quarters of a police force of a county.

willing to believe, I determined to canter on with my new acquaintances, the Seikh horse, leaving the Goorkhas in charge of the assistant magistrate, Mr. C——e. These Seikhs were evidently picked men; they were large, handsome fellows, generally well-dressed, but badly armed with matchlocks and all sorts of nondescript weapons, which, though it may have added to their picturesqueness, by no means gave me, on our first acquaintance, a very favourable impression of their working powers. Their costume, moreover, struck me as indicating a class of men intended rather for show than service; but, what was worse still, the horses, though evidently good, were by no means up to the weight of such lumping creatures. The endurance and metal, however, of these small half-bred Arabs, so utterly overweighted, afterwards often astonished me, and forced on me the conclusion that a small well-bred horse, even when overweighted, is more than a match for his larger brother, when constant hard work is required.

It was near midnight before we approached our destination. There was nothing in the appearance of the various villages, through which we thus unexpectedly passed, to indicate that any disturbance had taken place in their immediate vicinity—in a place, in fact, that they all looked up to as their capital. This carried with it the consolatory assurance that my calculations, founded on native veracity, had turned out correct; but, on approaching still closer, bungling through the intense darkness caused by an extensive grove of trees, after losing our path, we saw flames shooting up about a quarter of a mile in front, and at a considerable elevation above us, and we hurried on in the direction they indicated—a feat not accomplished without unhorsing some of our party in the deep watercuts, which it was impossible to distinguish. Coming close under the walls of the town, the absence of every human being from whom I had here expected to gather information, and, beyond the crackling of the flames, varied by the falling in of the walls of the houses, the deep, unnatural silence, struck me as very suspicious, and, for a moment or two, I thought that we had fallen into a trap; so we kept to the more open ground, till a confused old gentleman was discovered by a trooper contemplating his losses in the neighbourhood of his burning house. This poor creature seemed almost to have lost his senses; but through his agency, after considerable delay, the Thanahdar (chief police officer) was unearthed. From his report, which was also gloriously confused, it appeared that the rebels, with wonderful rapidity in their movements, after plundering and burning to their hearts' content, had scattered to their homes some couple of hours earlier. This actively determined energy surprised me to no small extent; but, distrusting the statement that the rebels had disappeared or dispersed, I took precautions accordingly.

The Tuhseelee and Thanah being on a considerable elevation, and not far removed from the outskirts of the town, I at once visited those places to ascertain if any of the public records could be saved; but both buildings, handsome of their kind, were hopelessly enveloped in flames, and soon fell to pieces. After posting men so as to prevent a surprise, and sending a party to conduct the Goorkhas in, on their arrival, I lay down in the centre of an open space within the Tuhseelee enclosure, where sleep, to my own astonishment afterwards, soon overtook me, in spite of the heated atmosphere, the result of the smouldering fires, and the constant crash of falling ruins all round. The infantry, as expected, did not appear for a very considerable time. Being convinced that, by instant pursuit, some of the attacking parties might be overtaken, I started as soon as the first glimmerings of morning made it possible to move over ground where I was still firmly convinced, in consequence of, to me, the unaccountable disappearance of the enemy, that a surprise was intended, as the rapidity of our arrangements in Saharunpore and march thence precluded the possibility of their receiving information of my advance even half an hour before my arrival. I had not at that time comprehended the generally strong objections of all natives to either engaging in any enterprise at night, or permitting such to be carried on after the close of day. This objection really arises from timidity—a feeling, in fact, that in the darkness unforeseen difficulties may arise, and that thus getting into a hobble at night,* escape might be by no means so easy. A Hindustani rarely fights at all without first examining carefully the chances of escape; hence, cavalry, in common with the Marhattas,† is always their favourite arm; the Seikh, on the other hand, prefers infantry, where his sturdy daring will always render him formidable.

The police and residents of the town of Nookur, when I discovered them, professing, from a mixture of ignorance, design, and fear, a total ignorance of the direction taken by their assailants, I was induced to determine on overhauling the country to our west, having noticed that we certainly had come across none of the vagabonds on the previous night, when advancing from the east, and I took it for granted that those villages, at any rate, were not concerned. In this conclusion I was wrong, however, as some of the very villages we had passed through, I subsequently ascertained, had been amongst the most active in this attack, and were eventually punished by me.

* This does not, however, apply to Indian thieves.

† This term Marhatta, or Mär-hutta, is derived from the mode of warfare adopted by these men. *Mär* means to strike, and *hûtna* to get out of the way; *i. e.*, those who struck a blow suddenly and at once retreated out of harm's way.

Our pursuit commenced at daybreak. To prevent mistakes, the thirty Goorkhas, placed under the charge of the assistant magistrate and Mr. W——s, a canal superintendent, were sent in a due westerly direction, where the ground was clear and open; while, accompanied by Mr. H——e, a clerk in the judge's office, I scoured the country with our small party of cavalry to see if any indications of the retreating marauders could be found. On one occasion, when obliged to follow the windings of an extensive jeel,* a considerable portion of which was deep and unfordable, we noticed a few hundred men collected under a village on the margin of the water, opposite the point where we were making an attempt to cross. It was by no means unnatural that the villagers should turn out to examine a party of troopers advancing in their direction, nor did any of us observe that they were armed.

Finding it impossible to ford at this point, we returned to hunt out a better spot. On this, the villagers fired several shots, beating their drums and shouting defiantly. This wild and uncalled-for demonstration of hostility was rather amusing than

* There is no term in English, that I know of, by which to translate this word. Jeel is essentially a tropical term; it refers to localities which for six months of the year, during and immediately after the monsoon rains, present the appearance of, and are in fact, lakes, but as the hot weather advances, dry up entirely or partially, becoming, in the latter case, marshes mixed with patches of clear water.

otherwise, as our original intentions towards this party were certainly peaceable enough. By keeping quiet on our first advance, the villagers might have wished to lull our suspicions with the intention of attacking, if we got into a mess when crossing; but if they thought we were actually retreating, one would suppose they would have been only too glad quietly to get rid of such ugly customers. We must conclude that Hindustani vanity and love of bravado could not resist this senseless demonstration. Knowing the Goorkhas could not be far off on the other side of the jeel, we cantered round, and after uniting with them advanced on the village, which we found tenantless, the courage of our assailants having evaporated. Being anxious to push on, in my contempt for the rascals, I did not disturb the domestic economy of their village, which I afterwards regretted when subsequent investigations enabled me to see their true character.

We advanced again in the same way we had started, and at last came upon a considerable party labouring along with their plunder, which, though close to their village, had unfortunately not been deposited in time. It was rather a novel scene to me from the vast amount of almost valueless property, such as doors, beams of wood, bundles of old clothes, &c., which these rascals were carrying away, though whatever was more valuable had probably been earlier secured in the village. I afterwards often noticed the same collections of almost worthless plunder; and it only shows what a curse these plundering tribes must have been, as they invariably set fire to or destroyed all that they could not carry off. In this mob of marauders I was hardly prepared to find many more women than men. Understanding the European treatment of women, the men, who were generally poorly armed, abandoning their plunder, scattered and attempted to escape, whilst the women stood still. In consequence of the small number of our troopers, the men were only too successful in effecting their escape, and a few only who attempted resistance were wounded, and the captured were fewer than they should have been; but it was a puzzle how to dispose of the large bevy of women, who stuck pertinaciously to their plunder.

A few troopers were now sent to summon the Goorkhas when we advanced on this village, also to find it, like the former, abandoned. A hundred troopers might have prevented the escape of the men, but our party was too small for this duty, where, as is almost always the case, extensive groves and scrub jungle surround the villages. The day was now far advanced, and we had gone a considerable distance from Nookur, so, collecting the recovered plunder, we made the prisoners, men and women, tramp back with double loads. This was the first instance I had observed of a practice universal among the Goojurs and other plundering tribes, that of being accompanied on their plundering excursions by their women, who are employed in assisting the other beasts of burden to carry off the plunder, and are probably rather good hands at discovering secreted property; hence, perhaps, the wonderful clearances made by these rascals in any place they attacked. On arriving at Nookur, the women were dismissed to their homes, as it was impossible for me to devise a good method of punishing them. We got back to our camp, men and horses well knocked up.

Finding on arrival that my former quarters amongst the ruins of the Tuhseelee were, in case of an attack, too confined by buildings and uncommonly hot, our small camp was removed to a fine grove of mangoe trees beyond the city, where good shelter from the sun existed. We had not finished a most welcome repast, when reports, each more threatening than the last, began to arrive by the men sent out to gather information. The whole country to a man had risen to attack us; nor was it possible to mistake the distant sound of the dhols, or drums, which they employed when summoning adherents or engaged in an attack, now familiar enough to all of us, and which were heard from every direction. It was a farce to suppose that our small band could resist a whole population, and Nookur was not a post there was any object in holding, now that all government property was destroyed. On a little reflection, however, it was clear that, though the

Europeans with the horse might easily escape, the thirty Goorkhas would be cut up to a man if a retreat was attempted: our plan, then, with such cowardly assailants was to stand on the defensive till reinforcements should arrive.

With this view I selected a high double brick-kiln,* not very far from our tents and nearly surrounded by water; to this we removed before the night closed in, leaving our camp standing to deceive the enemy, who had already entered some of the neighbouring groves. A number of coolies from the town of Nookur were rapidly collected, who, under Mr. W——s the canal sergeant's superintendence, formed a small breastwork at the only point where we could be easily assailed. In the meanwhile, one of our district horse-messengers had been despatched with a letter to Saharunpore, but being fired at, the useless fellow returned, though probably there was less danger in advancing than in retreating, while every little delay added to the difficulty of egress. I then despatched two others by different roads, ordering them for the first five or six miles, till they had evaded the circle occupied by the rebels, to take the Umballah direction, or the line of country exactly contrary to their destination. Another horseman

* From the peculiar manner in which bricks are manufactured in India, these brick-kilns always become considerable mounds, the excavations round them generally becoming large deep pools, at times almost lakes, of water.

was, when it grew darker, sent to Umbehtah to summon a certain Fureed Bux, a jemadar, or native officer, with his party of the 15th Irregulars, who had been there stationed to assist chiefly in the collection and transmission of the revenue. As mentioned before, we distrusted these 15th, but there was no help for it. The two horse-messengers I had last sent to Saharunpore might never reach their destination, while the Seikh troopers knew neither the country nor the language, and would be useless if required as messengers.

As it turned out, Fureed Bux at once obeyed my summons, and reached us at an early hour, much earlier, in fact, than I expected him. He reported that he had passed close to various bodies of rebels, who did not molest him, but he said things were looking serious. The arrival of this detachment from an unexpected quarter may have affected the movements of the rebels, if they ever would have had the pluck to carry out a determined attack on our small party, but, native-like, they contented themselves with plenty of noise, accompanied by constant firing and beating of drums, which continued without intermission throughout the night.

When ensconced on the brick-kiln, it became a difficult question where to station during the night both the 15th Irregulars and the Seikh cavalry. They could not assist in defending the neighbourhood of our position, the ground being too broken up for cavalry to act, nor could they come under or up to our little fort, so as to be under our protection. I was, therefore, obliged to order them to patrol between the tents and the brick-kiln during the night; and if a serious attack took place, to canter off all together, and send a party into Saharunpore, to make sure of reinforcements arriving. Both parties of cavalry seemed to me alarmed at this arrangement, particularly the Seikhs, the jemadar in command of whom did not conceal from me that he distrusted the 15th; the consequence was, that the Seikhs kept as close to us throughout the night as they could conveniently manage to do. My little friend, the Goorkha soobahdar, however, with his Nusseerees, entered into the spirit of the thing with a hearty good-will, suggesting and carrying out all kinds of small precautions or improvements in our fortification. Eventually we passed a very pleasant night together on the top of the brick-kiln, which no Hindustani enemy in the country would have found by any means easy to capture. As the morning dawned, we naturally began to reflect on the chances of either of the horse-messengers having reached their destination, as, if reasonably quick in their movements, our expected friends should soon be making their appearance. Their non-arrival would at any rate ensure us a jolly good baking throughout the day on the top of the brick-kiln, which is about as hot a position as could be selected.

The morning was advancing, and there had been a considerable lull in the noise around us, indicating, as we thought, an attack, when the welcome sound of regular file firing told us that the reinforcements were at hand, and some of our troopers soon galloped in, bringing the news of their advance. Before long, we exchanged greetings with Lieutenant Theo. B——n, whose ever-daring intelligence, during subsequent events, won the respect of all the Europeans present, while his firm tact endeared him to the men under his command. The party with which Lieutenant B——n now joined us consisted of some 130 Goorkhas of the Nusseeree Battalion, so that we now mustered 200 strong, of whom 70 were horse; the whole party being in good spirits and game for any encounter that might be anticipated in this direction.

CHAPTER VII.

Arrival of reinforcements under Lieutenant B——n—Rebels advance to attack us—Our movements—Engagement near Nookur—A turban an important protection against sword-cuts—Gallantry of Mr. Hyde—Imperfection in the English soldier's rifle—Importance of a perfect weapon in India—Punishment inflicted on rebel prisoners—Universality of the revolt in this tract—Our line of action in consequence—Futtua proclaimed King of the Goojurs—The Ranghurs of Khoondah—March to attack Futtua on the night of the 24th of June—Expected ambush and tedious advance—Opening of the monsoon—Unpleasant position in company with the 15th Irregulars—Fired at from the village of Mohunpore—The place attacked—Advance on Boodha Kheree—Goorkhas at a well—Halt at Gungoh—Night march on the 26th of June—Advance to attack Khoondah—Engagement at Oomerpore—Anecdote of a Goorkha on horseback—Cruelty of the Goorkhas as a race—Enmity between the 15th Irregulars and the Goorkhas—Rajah of Putteeala's body-guard and the 15th Irregulars—Perfect discipline maintained by the latter—History of the 15th—Their imprisonment and release—March to Rampore—Friendliness of the rebels we had defeated—Character of the Bunyahs—Disastrous consequences of our legal provisions for the recovery of small debts; Sunthal rebellion one of its results; discontent throughout the North-West Provinces from the same cause—The villagers at Manpore join in the murder of English ladies and children—Their conduct a result of the action of our civil courts.

I HAVE mentioned that we heard firing on the approach of our reinforcement, in explanation of which it appeared that Lieutenant B——n had been attacked near Nookur by some 200 of the rebels, whom he dispersed, capturing the zemindar of Sundowlee—one of their leaders—and killing some ten or twelve of the attacking party. Lieutenant B——n had hardly arrived at our encampment, when information was brought that a large body of men were advancing from the opposite direction to that in which he had come, and all prepared accordingly. A long succession of groves existed in the direction from which the rebels were advancing, and Lieutenant B——n determined to take advantage of this cover for the infantry, while I was to keep out in the open country with our horse, and, if possible, draw the enemy on to the infantry. I knew where the infantry were to be found, but saw nothing more of them for some time. On rounding the groves we found ourselves, as we had anticipated, on the borders of a considerable plain; and, a little to our surprise, we were here confronted by a large body of men, drawn up in line with considerable regularity, some four or five deep, with horsemen riding up and down the line to keep it in proper order. The line was a very extended one, and was advancing slowly and steadily till we came out on them, when all at once they halted. It was not my object to stop their advance, so, after looking at each other for a few minutes without exchanging a shot, I ordered my men to retreat slowly. The moment this retrograde movement commenced, a cheer was set up and carried along the whole line. At the same time they gave us a volley, and it was surprising that the result was only one casualty on our side, as the bullets certainly came thick enough.

My party was separated from Lieutenant B——n and the Goorkhas by a seesoo grove, so we could not observe what was going on there; but the rebels continuing their advance, received a volley from the Goorkhas, which divided their line into two large confused masses, and this being succeeded by a rapid advance and pursuit, the rebels scattered all over the plain. My previous policy had not, it was clear, been severe enough, otherwise this revolt would never have assumed its present proportions, and, considering that in the end it would be the most humane course, I to-day determined to act with greater severity in the pursuit, however disagreeable at times this became. Few prisoners were taken, but it was a satisfaction to feel that no innocent man could be killed. The plain was an extensive one, from which the nearest villages were some three or four miles distant. No man was present on that plain that day but had come a considerable distance from his home to oppose the government authority, and the troopers could here be trusted with full licence.

The rebels on this occasion had evidently become over-confident in the superiority of their numbers; either they were ignorant of the arrival of Lieutenant B——n's relieving party, or they must have possessed utter fools as leaders, otherwise they never would have advanced across an open plain, risking an encounter on a spot where in case of defeat they were sure of a cruel cutting up, whereas they might have given infinite trouble by keeping to the trees and underwood. This day a practical illustration was given to me of the important protection that a large thick turban opposes to sword cuts. From ignorance on this point I found Mr. Hyde in considerable difficulty; he had been attacked, and making a cut at his opponent on the head, the blow shivered his own sword, but did not injure his assailant.

Mr. Hyde, I may here observe, was a clerk in the judge's office. A gallantly daring and humane combatant, no transient excitement tempted him to inflict unnecessary injury. This, it may be supposed, is no great virtue; but men in the position of the Europeans at that time in Northern India, when the desperation of their situation rendered recklessness of life a *sine quâ non*, if English supremacy was to be maintained at all, and who habitually staked their lives day after day, could hardly be expected, when in the midst of those scenes, to hold so sacred the lives of their enemies in a war proclaiming extermination to Europeans. Those scenes which a stern necessity had forced upon us were sadly demoralizing to all engaged. I could not consequently but admire this man, then but in the position of a clerk, always in the fore-rank, and who invariably checked, aye despised, the slightest exhibition of hatred to a race who were still slaughtering English women and children, and had destroyed all the little patrimony he possessed in the world.

The immense number of shots that were fired both by the enemy and ourselves without effect in this encounter surprised me; but I afterwards observed quite as bad practice among European regiments armed with the far-famed Minié. To me it consequently ceased to be a subject of astonishment how battles were decided by the bayonet, for previously, as one of the uninitiated, I never could understand how such close engagements could take place considering the storm of bullets that had to be met. The English soldier is now supplied with a beautiful rifle, perfect so far as regards its capabilities of range and correctness, but a trigger is added so stiff and unmanageable that it becomes next to useless in the hands of the best shot in the world. The stiff trigger is supplied as a safeguard against accidents, but it is also a secure enough guarantee that the enemy be not injured. A sportsman seldom meets with an accident, however fine the trigger of his rifle may be set; why, then, should not the soldier, whose profession is supposed to be that of arms, arrive at something near the same perfection? As he is always fingering and shouldering his weapon, surely this carelessness could be cured. Let the soldier have the fine trigger, but whenever he is obliged to carry his musket on duty, make him carry it capped, and loaded with blank cartridge. Any accidental explosions would be of little consequence, but punish the soldier smartly if they occur. In a short time he would learn to handle his weapon so as not to be dangerous to his friends. This would entail a slight additional expense on Government both in the trigger and blank cartridges, but the money would be well spent. A body of men would thus be prepared for the hour of battle, by far more formidable than they are likely to prove so long as the present trigger is in use. Every possible superiority in the construction of the English soldier's arms becomes a paramount necessity in India, where the European has to contend with such vast numbers, and no better illustration could exist of its importance than the terror with which the rebels invariably regarded the English gentleman's rifle.*

* In India, as a matter of self-defence, the possession of a practically useful pistol will always be of considerable importance. In the common average-sized revolving pistol I found that the balls were much too small. A mortal wound might be inflicted on an opponent; but at the moment he hardly felt it, and continued the attack as if only receiving an extra spur. But even in the common Colt's pistol, then a valued friend, this mistake was, to a certain extent, rectified by ordering a village iron-smith to form a mould, which produced a ball in the shape of a plug filling up the whole of the chamber. No inconvenience arose from thus filling up the chamber; while this long plug inflicts a much more fatal wound than the spherical ball. The object, generally, of the possessor of a pistol is not the death of an assailant, for which purpose the smaller spherical ball might eventually be sufficient, but it is to check his course and prevent him inflicting a wound. To effect this object a ball of under three-quarters of an ounce in weight is

On the evening of the day succeeding our return from the encounter near Nookur, I hanged, in the arch of the ruined gateway attached to the Government Tuhseelee, a leading rebel, who had assisted in its destruction, and who had been captured by Lieutenant B——n during his advance the previous morning.* The prisoners brought in by myself a couple of days earlier, being insignificant men, were dismissed to their homes after receiving a sufficiently

almost useless, but the more conical or plug-shaped the ball is formed, consistently with strength, the better, as, for the same weight of metal, its effects will be more instantaneous in paralysing an assailant. In Indian terai, or forest, shooting, where the undergrowth of jungle, grass, and thorny scrub generally affords an impenetrable cover close at hand, I have often noticed animal after animal escaped when the most fatal shots had been delivered with the spherical ball, while few escaped from the conical ball of the same weight, even though it may have originally entered in by no means so fatal a locality. Again, the self-cocking pistols are almost valueless. The slight difference of rapidity with which the fire is delivered is practically an object not for a moment to be compared to steady correctness of aim. One carefully aimed shot, even amongst a crowd of assailants, will go infinitely farther towards protecting life than half-a-dozen discharges from the self-cocking pistol, with which it is impossible to take an aim when at all hurried. An almost hair-trigger is no trivial advantage, particularly when mounted; while the barrels of pistols are generally made too long for securing a rapid aim; and in a weapon to be used at close quarters it is difficult to discover the object of such length. A heavy ball, short barrel, and a fine trigger, are the three important points in a pistol as a weapon of self-defence.

* As a magistrate, I only possessed the power of imprisonment to the extent of three years, so that it became a considerable stretch of authority to assume the power of passing capital sentences, on which I ever after acted, when unable to collect enough officers to form a court-martial; but necessity is sadly illegal, for,

severe flogging to prevent them reappearing in arms for some time. On the day succeeding this we attacked certain other rebellious villages which, on investigation, had proved to have been principals in this insurrection.

Revolt had now become universal throughout this tract, and it became a question which body of rebels ought to be first dealt with as likely to ensure the best chance of overawing the rest into submission; our force being too small to entertain a hope of the possibility of reaching all our enemies. A certain Futtua, of Boodha Kheree, distant some fifteen miles, had proclaimed himself King of the Goojurs, and had been generally acknowledged as such. Beyond him existed a more formidable enemy in the Ranghurs of Khoondah and its vicinity. Ranghurs are a caste of Mahomedan Rajpoots, converted by force from Hindooism in the good old days of the Mahomedan emperors. These men have now become extremely bigoted Mahomedans, and for Hindustanis are generally good and brave horsemen. Less important bands and individuals were in revolt both to our east and west; but it was determined to attack these, the most powerful, at once. These Ranghurs

girt with revolt, there was no one with whom I could possibly correspond capable of conferring this power upon me, and we knew not even of the existence of the penal Acts passed by the Supreme Council during the revolt till the lapse of many months after they became law. Application for sanction was, however, once made, but the reply was never received; in all probability it highly edified the rebels.

inhabited portions of the Khâdir, or low alluvial lands, on the left bank of the Jumna. There was every indication that the monsoon, with the tropical rains, would soon commence, and this Khâdir land of the Jumna would then become inaccessible, so that we had no time to lose, it being important to make these men feel our power before it would become possible for them to defy us in a country that would rapidly be transformed into a vast swamp.

About one or two A.M., on the 24th of June, we started to surprise, if possible, Futtua, the King of the Goojurs, whose dominions lay between us and the Ranghurs of Khoondah. We had been marching along quietly for some time, when I received information that the rebels had anticipated our move, and that a large body of men were lying in ambush either in or near a village we had attacked the previous day, and through which we must again pass. Lieutenant B——n now called a halt, and made a different disposition of our force. It was an intensely dark night, with heavy clouds rolling up from the south-west, a sure indication of the opening of the monsoon. I had gone on with rather a strong reconnoitring party — strong, I mean, considering our force—but the trees and underwood, added to the darkness, rendered our advance very slow. By this time we had surrounded the place; but the rebels had evacuated it, and, by the flashes of lightning, we saw several bodies of men moving off. Beyond a shot or two—fired to elicit, if possible, a reply, and thus ascertain the position of their main body—nothing came of the surprise; our object, however, was to push on to Boodha Kheree.

The morning broke gloriously; the deep massive clouds vividly illuminated with those brilliantly delicate tints so often characteristic of the setting in and closing of the monsoon. Though in India, if exposed to much rain, the results may be by no means pleasant, we all hailed with joy the delightful change of temperature, after the dry, parching heat at the termination of the hot season. This transition put us all in good spirits; but the 15th Irregulars, who formed a portion of my party, could hardly be said to have promoted the exhilarating tendency. When riding along with me, the jemadar and others constantly questioned me, rather too familiarly, as to the ultimate result of their loyalty; their object being to make me commit myself to some definite promise. Most disagreeably in their power, I was in a manner put on my defence, and had to employ my time in warding off those cleverly put questions, not one of which could I possibly fix upon as pointedly disloyal, though anxious enough to bring the discussion to a close; but a few stray shots fortunately changed the subject of our conversation, and when the Seikhs with the Goorkhas joined us this disagreeable incident was at an end.

My advanced party had been proceeding rather

slowly for the main body to make up with us, when, passing under the rather large village of Mohunpore, surrounded by a mud wall, we were fired upon, receiving at the same time a direct challenge to attack the place. These villagers may have concluded that the force before them was all that would be brought against the village, as the rest of our party were not in sight. Keeping clear of bullet range, while preventing with the troopers as far as was possible any egress from the place we halted till the advent of Lieutenant B——n with the main body, when we attacked the place, which again unfortunately caused considerable delay, and these constant interruptions disappointed all our hopes of surprising Futtua's party, who had totally abandoned their town, which was a defensible one, and rather well built.

The beautiful groves surrounding Boodha Kheree, with its commanding position, and the prosperous appearance of the whole scene, impressed me forcibly with the infatuation of a man in the position of Futtua, possessing a considerable stake in the country, and surrounded also by those comforts and appliances most valued by natives. Boodha Kheree was one of those spots now and then met with in the North-West Provinces beyond the influence of the Himalayas, where one is occasionally reminded that nature has not entirely abandoned those vast plains to their undeviating sameness, and has to a slight extent broken through the dead uniformity of the landscape. During the afternoon, when seated near a well at Boodha Kheree, from which the Goorkhas not on duty were drawing water, I was struck by their insisting on my drinking out of their own drinking vessels. This a Hindoo, and more especially the hill Rajpoots, the class from which these men are recruited, will never permit; and it was evident that the Goorkhas, recovering their loyalty, were determined by every device they could think of to show that they had no longer any sympathy for the false-caste outcry into which they had been themselves so nearly drawn. By the evening of the 24th of June we reached Gungoh, a rather important town, to protect which was partly our object in coming in this direction. Here we halted a day to give the men a little rest, and to enable me to gather information regarding the Khoondah Ranghurs, which being effected, a little after midnight, early on the 26th of June, we commenced our march with the view of attacking these insurgents.

Though I was familiar with the cross roads, we experienced a little difficulty towards morning in finding our way and keeping together. To prevent information being carried to the rebels, guides had been dispensed with, but the enemy were fully prepared to oppose us in considerable force, drawn up in line on the slope of a hill at the village of Oomerpore, several miles in advance of Khoondah. After crossing a small, deep backwater of the Jumna, running under Lucknoutee, I had gone ahead at Lieutenant B——n's request with a few horse, to ascertain where the enemy were to be found; and, on approaching this ground, received a volley from some men posted amongst groves in front of the position taken up by the rebels. On this I rejoined Lieutenant B——n, and we all advanced in two columns; and after a smart exchange of fire we closed with the rebels, and, routing them, continued the pursuit until they entered some dâkh jungle. We then turned to our right and advanced on Khoondah itself, where the enemy again opposed us. In both these encounters our losses were only a Seikh trooper and a Goorkha wounded, and one horse killed, though the rebels suffered severely, particularly in the pursuit.*

A Goorkha was the subject of a most ludicrous scene at Khoondah. One of the enemy's horse being well mounted, thought fit to come rather too close; a couple of Goorkhas knelt down, fired, and the man fell. They ran up to secure the horse, which was caught, but would not be led. Determined not to lose their prize, one mounted him, but could not abandon his arms. The horse did not approve. He kicked and reared, but being unable to throw his rider, made off towards his retreating companions.

* For the military view of these encounters, *vide* Appendix, p. 234.

Here was our friend, who had in all probability never before in his lifetime mounted a horse, careering across country, holding on to the mane by one hand, to his musket and fixed bayonet with the other, his various collections of nondescript articles gradually leaving his care to adorn the plain. Some of our horsemen, however, headed the refractory steed, and drove the Goorkha back to his companions amid general merriment. Rarely could a more ludicrous sight, combined with more downright pluck, be witnessed, for the residents of the Himalayas know not what a horse is. There is so much dash and activity in a Goorkha that, in spite of being mountaineers, no more formidable body of light horse could be raised than a Goorkha regiment or two. I would rather have one such to follow me than two or three Hindustanis or Seikhs.

After the capture of Khoondah we found many women had been destroyed by throwing themselves down wells and into the Jumna. It was a melancholy fact, but could not have been averted by any precautions within our control, so absolutely without doubt in the native mind is the treatment women are led to expect and invariably receive from natives into whose hands the fortune of war has placed them, that it becomes a point of honour with a virtuous native woman on such occasions to destroy herself rather than become a prisoner. One unfortunate woman in particular was noticed in a court-yard that must soon be enveloped in flames; she was standing with her children, heedless of the calls of a party of Goorkhas to come out. The poor creature being evidently frightened, I ordered the Goorkhas not to enter, and removed the children myself; but it being impossible to induce the woman to move of her own accord, and as there was no time to spare, I caught hold of her to take her out. I had no idea that she was so wildly frightened as turned out to be the case, or I should have taken good care she could not escape; she managed, however, by a quick turn, to leave the clothes which I had hold of with me, and dashed into the burning portion of the court-yard. I did not see her again, though she may have escaped, but not without severe injuries.

Though the Nusseerees at their advent hardly possessed a cheerful character, and had doubtless been at one time irresolute, the influence of class precedent, which had hurled all Hindustanis into revolt, guided their course also. These men saw that their countrymen, the Sirmourees, had risked all in our cause, had made the Hindustanis their enemies,* and were fighting nobly at Delhi. The Nusseerees now determined to range themselves on the side of their countrymen and ours, setting about it with

* Which would never have been the case if Hindustanis and Goorkhas had been mixed in the same regiments, an improvement which is now proposed.

the usual enthusiasm of mountaineers. To restrain them became the only difficulty. Constantly did they reiterate to me that the Mahomedans were our real enemies, and by way of showing affection, on all occasions did they ill-treat every Mahomedan they could get hold of quietly; and these Mahomedans, with wonderful want of foresight and ignorance of Goorkha character, constantly taunted and irritated them.

The Goorkhas, in evincing their zeal, certainly impressed the people with great dread; they were at one time even represented as cannibals. During one march, a country bumpkin, who had been of some trifling service to a Goorkha, thought he had ingratiated himself sufficiently to broach a most momentous question. According to Hindustani etiquette, permission to speak was duly requested and granted. With fear and trembling he then inquired whether it was really true that there was a man-eater among them? "True," responded the Goorkha, "I am the man." The astonished bumpkin shrunk back, not to be seen again; the Goorkha party enjoying the joke, as demonstrated by the usual true Indo-Chinese grin.

In common with all Goorkhas, these men were deeply cruel by nature, and in their anxiety to evince loyalty, this propensity was prominent enough. I remember on one occasion making a few prisoners; telling off some of the 15th Irregulars to guard them,

I galloped on; but I had not gone far when I heard a disturbance behind me. On looking back it was evident that a strong party of Goorkhas were disputing violently with the horsemen. Knowing the enmity kindled, for the well-being of both parties I galloped back to restrain them; but the Goorkhas were too strong for the troopers, and too quick for me. The prisoners were seized from the horsemen, and decapitated with kookeries as coolly as if their executioners were engaged in their favourite occupation of thus disposing of a devoted goat. On hearing my remonstrance, they replied to me as to a child, and with almost scornful contempt informed me that if I did not yet understand how to rule Hindustanis, they at any rate did; that if the Europeans insisted, with their usual insane weakness, in sparing Hindustanis, they would simply be kicked out of the country. With the enemy in front, discussion was short, so we proceeded and separated in the pursuit.

The ill-will, however, between the Goorkhas and the 15th Irregulars very nearly led to blows hardly an hour later. I had gone ahead with the 15th to cut off the retreat of some of the enemy; the rebels retraced their steps when we got successfully to their rear, and the Goorkhas in pursuit advanced firing. Many of their shots coming amongst us, my men were irritated. I showed them that this could hardly be avoided, when most of them subsided into sullen respectfulness; but some insolent fellows seized the first opportunity, when Lieutenant B——n came in sight, to intimate to him that they would have a fight if he did not keep his Goorkhas in hand. They were rather taken aback, however, when quietly informed that he also was quite "game" for the encounter, and we heard no more on the subject. Throughout these encounters I observed how comparatively well armed all the rebels seemed to be; but the majority of the matchlocks captured had been recently manufactured, which accounted for their owners proving themselves such bad marksmen. This circumstance also shows the rapidity with which Hindustanis, even common villagers, adopt the manufacture of arms.

The Hindustani and Seikh Horse, here mentioned as forming a portion of our force, were a curious contrast to each other. The Seikhs were large, handsome men, who looked well and very picturesque on horseback, but rarely, when required, unless well looked after, did they come to the front. Their bad armament, which I noticed they felt bitterly when in company with the 15th Irregulars, was probably one reason; but though Seikhs may make poor cavalry, as infantry they would thrash all the other races in India put together. The 15th Irregulars, composed chiefly of Hindustani Mahomedans, were light, good riders, with a great deal of dash, but no real pluck; I never saw them perform an unmistakeably plucky action. When in action, however, the Hindustanis were always well up, while at times I could hardly find out where the Seikhs got to. This was the more annoying, as I could not trust the Irregulars, particularly some fellows that invariably kept close to me.

But never did soldiers more perfectly maintain their drill under adverse circumstances than these 15th Irregulars, and more effectively armed no cavalry regiment could be. A jemadar was the highest native officer amongst them, and he issued all the orders to the men, as I knew nothing of military nomenclature. My orders to the jemadar, though unmistakeable in meaning, were anything but military. In spite of this ignorance on my part, which amongst Europeans might have elicited contempt, all maintained their discipline, combined, generally, with the most respectful obedience, and they carried out the movements required of them as perfectly as my non-military eye ever observed on a parade ground. These men behaved loyally as long as they were with me, but cost me many an anxious hour when alone in their company. Often have I ridden along contemplating how many I could manage to shoot down before they extinguished me; while now and then they must have observed that I was watching the direction of their carbines. The Goorkhas hated these 15th most satisfactorily; but not so the Seikhs, who, in the event of the 15th mutinying, would, I am certain, have looked quietly on; still, as being neutral, they tended more, I suspect, to keep the 15th to their work than if they had been demonstratively loyal to the English cause. The Seikhs became, in fact, a valuable connecting link; the Hindustani as well as ourselves could depend on them for a certain passive friendliness not to be despised by either party.

A little before my departure from the Saharunpore district, and long after the fall of Delhi, these 15th Irregulars were sent to do duty with a detachment of Seikh and Affghan horse, who were watching the fords of the Ganges, patrolling the right bank of the river in the Mozuffurnugur district. There, with the usual Hindustani incomprehensibleness, some of the 15th deserted to the enemy during a trifling encounter with the enemy's pickets, and the rest were imprisoned by the commanding officer, though subsequently, when unable to work mischief, they were released on account of their previous good conduct. These men then, not unlike the 29th Native Infantry, also at Saharunpore, having done good service throughout a period when they might have mutinied with impunity, and when all was apparently against us, after all doubt had disappeared even from the native mind as to the ultimate victors in the contest, chose to throw off their allegiance.

After leaving the vicinity of Khoondah, we returned at once to our camp at Gungoh, and the following night the rains, which had threatened us for some time, set in in earnest. In consequence of apprehensions of attack in other directions, we gradually wended our way, *viâ* Rampore, which had been threatened by the rebels, to the station of Saharunpore. The country was now flooded, and our progress consequently slow. Such, however, had been the effect of the severe lessons given to the Goojurs and Ranghurs, that throughout our marches the country people were delighted to see us, and met us as if old friends, with presents of milk, cakes, &c. This was the more amusing, as some of the most liberal of our new allies had been engaged against us in the encounter near Nookur, though, doubtless, not aware that we were acquainted with the fact; but we all soon became the best of friends, nor did this tract of country ever give any more trouble.

Such investigations as it was possible to make during constant marching night and day, at a season of the year when, with the shelter of a good house, ordinary existence is considered hard enough, proved that the Mahomedans in this tract were throughout the instigators to revolt. They had risen as a body, and the Hindoos who swelled their ranks, rendering the rising universal, were almost all of that class who would gain by anarchy and the destruction of the records of their debts, and that this latter inducement to revolt was one of their keenest relishes during these disturbances it was easy to observe. In attacking Nookur, for instance, and I observed it afterwards in other places, they were not content to burn or destroy the bunyahs'* houses and property and throw the accounts into the flames—this would have been a too rapid termination of their delights—but the account-books were carried out of the town with them, and torn up in the surrounding gardens and highways. In some instances this even was not sufficient, as the track of parties could now and then be followed for a couple of miles or more, who had wandered along strewing the scattered remains of their prizes along the line of country they had taken. The creditors of the poorer class of cultivators invariably inhabit the larger towns, so that these towns, naturally enough, became a point of attack when the civil power was paralysed.

In these irruptions, the quarter in the towns inhabited by the Mahomedans was never attacked by the villagers, nor did the Mahomedans join the townspeople in measures of resistance, which would seem to indicate that an understanding existed between the villagers and the Mahomedans. Still the latter not being generally very rich and likely to fight well in defence of their property, may have operated as strong inducements to the villagers not to molest them, or previously, perhaps,

* Dealers in corn and lenders of money.

to enter into easy terms with them, which the Mahomedans considered it not only prudent, but advantageous to accept, as likely to clear off at the same time all records of their own debts in the money-lenders' possession.

Appreciating, as natives do, English justice and honesty in general, there is nothing amongst the agricultural population that creates a greater hatred of our rule than the facilities offered to the most unprincipled class of money-lenders in the world in oppressing an ignorant and careless peasantry. The debts of all classes, but particularly of the poorer, are incurred by their barbarous extravagance at festivals—marriages, births, &c.—and any legitimate check imposed by the Government on such extravagance would be a blessing to the people, and would be received as such. This check, both to the extravagance of the peasantry and the crushing adroitness of the money-lender, so often proposed by men interested in the welfare of the natives in the North-West Provinces, but opposed by lawyers, is merely to withdraw all legal remedy for the recovery of small debts, say to the amount of 500 rupees (*50l.*), and it may be worthy of consideration to determine whether, with the knowledge of the origin of the Sunthal insurrection before us, we are content to incur the hatred of the mass of the manly population of a subject country, in order that the most cowardly and ungrateful moneyed class on the face of the earth may spring into existence, for a bunyah glories* in physical and moral decrepitude, exhibiting not the slightest shame in confessing that he is less able to protect himself than a woman; and I have seen one look upon me as nearly insane, and consider himself a highly injured individual, when it was suggested to him that he might, at any rate, have attempted to defend his own person and property when attacked.

The bunyah, too, when he purchases the land, never dreams of living on or improving it. In England, the question of the bankrupt landholder and the capitalist soon resolves itself, for both belong to the same race, and the latter can confer greater benefits on the land than the former, so that the capitalist assumes the position of a landholder with every advantage to the country; but in India we have two almost quite distinct races, and we, as conquerors, by legislating so as to ensure the ruin of the manlier class, only advance in his place feeble vermin, unable to crawl without our support, so that we can be hardly surprised if, in the hour of danger, we discover that we possess no

* Bunyahs, or Mahaguns, shopkeepers and bankers, who are in reality but different grades of the same class of money-lenders, are totally distinct from the rest of the population in the North-West Provinces, though Brahmuns and one or two other castes do sometimes attempt, with no great success, the occupation of shopkeeping and money-lending.

friends at all capable of assisting us. It is also worthy of remark that, when investigating cases of rebellion on our reoccupation of the country, I found that no class seem to have acted with so vindictive a hate against us as the smaller class of landholders whom the bunyahs had dispossessed through the medium of our courts. In one notorious case, the murder of forty Europeans, chiefly ladies and children, near Manpore, on the Ganges, three-fourths of the villagers who joined the sepoys in this wholesale murder, and without whose assistance the sepoys would have been powerless, were dispossessed landholders of the smaller class, and many of them Brahmuns, a caste who rarely joined in such deeds.

CHAPTER VIII.

Mutiny of the detachment of the 29th Native Infantry—Conduct of the Rajah of Putteeala's body-guard—The welcome departure of the 29th—Power of our courts and police during the revolt—Rise of the Bunjarahs in the Khâdir of the Ganges—Departure for Roorkie accompanied by the Putteeala Seikhs—Agent of the Jwallapore Raos—Situation of Futtuah, the head-quarters of the Bunjarahs—Importance of rapidity in our movements—Our force at starting—March along the banks of the Ganges Canal—Encampment at Jwallapore—Astonishment of the natives at the universal arming of the Europeans—Their fondness for intrigue—Its supposed advantages—March to attack Futtuah—Desolation of the country—Former ravages of the Goorkhas—Climate of the Khâdir—The Bangunga unfordable—Encampment at Ranee Majra—Attack made by the Bunjarahs—The contingent furnished by the Jwallapore Raos—Their armament and conduct—Passage of the Bangunga—A wounded Bunjarâh—Advance on Futtuah—Rebels retreat to an island in the Ganges—Their plundered corn and cattle—Return to Roorkie.

After our return from the Nookur and Khoondah expedition, all remained tolerably quiet till the 11th of July. Several natives had given timely information that our treasury guard, the detachment of the 29th Native Infantry, intended to mutiny on the evening of the 11th, but the warning was unheeded, or, as usual, discredited. It was not considered fitting to disarm them, though the Goorkhas would have been delighted with the diversion. We were all seated at dinner when the news already anticipated by several arrived. Information was brought from Captain M——l's house that the small guard stationed there, in charge of the treasure chest, usually kept at the stud superintendent's house, had abandoned their post, and joined the main body of the 29th, at the civil treasury, on the opposite side of the river. We were in the midst of a conversation on the subject, so that all were prepared for action, though too late.

The Goorkhas, encamped in the grounds surrounding the neighbouring house, were at once ordered under arms, and the officers left for their respective posts. Captain M——l, in charge of the stud, went over to one of his own barracks, or extensive lines of stables, in which the stud horses were kept, and where the Putteeala Rajah's body-guard were temporarily quartered, to get these men under arms, while I, after completing some necessary arrangements, rode over to see how my friends were progressing. Captain M——l had found these Seikhs almost immovable, and my former experience of them was destined to be sadly disappointed. To get them under arms was no easy matter; this thing or that was wanting, or out of order; and it soon became evident that the delay was intentional, as, indeed, one of the men afterwards confessed, stating that a promise had been given not to molest the

29th, if it were possible by any means to avoid doing so. In spite, then, of all our efforts, they managed to waste so much time before declaring themselves ready to move, that when we joined the Goorkhas, and the whole force moved on, it was evident to all that, in an intensely dark, rainy night, such as this was, we should never see anything more of the 29th.

A cautious advance brought us to the cutchery whence the sepoys had vanished. They had left all in the treasury room untouched, and abandoned much of their own private property in their lines; so that their desertion, though premeditated, was eventually hurriedly carried out. Two men, to all appearance accidentally, though I suspect wilfully, remained behind at the post-office guard, and were the next day dismissed to their homes. One of these had a wife and child with him in the lines; the other, to my astonishment, was the very man, a Chutree, who, of the whole detachment of sepoys, had been the most insolent and violent to me at Khera. Natives, in speaking to me, frequently said that the 29th had no wish to mutiny with violence, but intended to follow the gentlemanly example of their own regiment. When the head-quarters of this regiment mutinied, they behaved extremely well; they had secured a safe retreat, not only to their own officers, but also to all the European residents of Moradabad who chose to depart within the time granted.

Nevertheless, my former experience of the violence of the men of this detachment at Khera was far from conducive to a sense of security whilst engaged at office work, with a guard of the 29th surrounding the cutchery. Here, with only a carefully concealed revolver, it would be impossible to resist with any chance of success. It was, moreover, necessary to assume an appearance of complete confidence, possessed by none present, not even by the native Omlah, many of whom, particularly the Bengalees, had almost as much reason to dread an outbreak as ourselves. The very visit to cutchery amounted to a farce, so far, at least, as respects the actual transaction of ordinary district duties. Still, though uncomfortable to Europeans, and the natives themselves requiring no such assistance, the short visits to cutchery were probably beneficial, as showing that we were determined to hold our own. Disputes were then settled more summarily than by a reference to the magistrate; might was right; travelling to any distance from their homes would only have ensured the destruction either of the wanderer or of any members of his family unable to protect themselves, or dependent upon him for protection. Every man's hand was against his neighbour, and an attempt to complain in a Furinghee* court would have been resented with total annihilation. After all, the appellant would only have appeared in a mock court,

* Furinghee, "English," but employed as a term of contempt.

as our police were powerless; no native dreamt of obeying them; they lived in their police stations on sufferance alone, and learnt to behave themselves accordingly.

Since the Nusseerees had shown clearly which side they had taken, we cared little how the 29th behaved. To those, however, destined to attend cutchery, the departure of the troops was a relief, for even had we disarmed them, it would have been necessary to dismiss them to their homes, as we could not have spared the men to watch them. Our chief regret was, that they had not left their arms. The morning after their disappearance, I started with the Putteeala Horse for that portion of the district east of Roorkie, termed the Khâdir, or low alluvial deposits of the Ganges, which had shown a fancy to take its turn of rebellion; and, on arriving at Roorkie, found Captain R——d, commanding the station, in possession of intelligence that the Bunjarahs had entrenched themselves at Futtuah. This was not improbable, as a number of the sappers, who had mutinied at Roorkie, were then supposed to be in the Khâdir of the Ganges, and to be the instigators of the alleged movement.

With every wish to assist me, the only force the Roorkie party could add to my Putteeala Horse was from thirty to forty sappers, who had remained loyal at the time of the mutiny of the two companies to which they belonged. There was also one old honeycombed gun, a nine-pounder, manned by three or four Europeans. At the request of Captain R——d, I sent to Saharunpore for some fifty Goorkhas, where, all seeming likely to remain quiet, it appeared probable they might be spared; but others were of a different opinion, and my demand was refused. It now became a question whether it would be prudent, considering the information we had received, to risk a distant expedition with the force at our disposal. Just at this time, a karindah, or agent, from the Raos of Jwallapore, called on me. He came to ask for assistance, as the Bunjarahs had plundered and burnt a number of his master's villages, and threatened an attack on Jwallapore itself, which is an important and wealthy town. The Raos were Mahomedans, and could not be entirely trusted, being intimate friends of the rebel Nawab of Nujeebabad, the ruler of the left bank of the Jumna, but they were, for the time, evidently alarmed; being, moreover, Rajpoot Mahomedans, and hated by the cow-adoring Bunjarahs, they might actually assist me as much as it was possible for me to aid them. When the agent, then, pressed my visiting Jwallapore, I not unwillingly promised to do so, on condition that the Raos should furnish a contingent of at least a hundred men to assist in attacking the Bunjarahs. This the agent readily agreed to do, and left.

Futtuah, the head-quarters of the Bunjarahs, was

in a direct line not more than thirty miles from Roorkie; but the rains had commenced, and the whole of the low country intervening was under water, and being intersected by innumerable streams, now all flooded, this tract of country was perfectly impassable to any but the Bunjarahs themselves. Our shooting expeditions had made us acquainted with the fact, that rather an elevated ridge ran towards Futtuah from Jwallapore. The favour made of the trip to the north, when wishing to proceed due east, was consequently more apparent than real. The circuit by Jwallapore had become absolutely necessary. Captain R——d, commanding at Roorkie, at once saw the necessity of rapidity in our movements, and gave every man he could spare, though the number of ladies and children in Roorkie rendered it necessary to leave a sufficient force, particularly of Europeans, for their protection. Time being of importance, we could not wait for the chance of eventually obtaining the Goorkhas. Delay might induce the Bijnour rebels to cross the Ganges and join the Bunjarahs, in which case our force might, even with the Goorkhas, be insufficient to cope with the enemy.

Our army, at starting from Roorkie, consisted of from thirty to forty Hindustani sappers, with one engineer officer in charge, another engineer officer in charge of the gun, my Putteeala Horse, and several European volunteers, including the geological professor, with two or three students of the Thomason College—rather a curious mixture, but all Europeans, whatever their profession, now necessarily turned into fighting animals. On the 3rd of July, everything being ready, the start was made. The troops left in the morning by a rather long, but comparatively dry, native track to the north-west of the Ganges Canal. An engineer officer and myself determined to start later and meet our friends at Jwallapore, by a more direct road, along the left bank of the Ganges Canal. Having myself a good deal to arrange regarding the revenue collections prior to starting, we were unfortunately rather late in doing so.

I had never before passed along this portion of the Ganges Canal, and was much struck with the extent and importance of the works rendered necessary by the natural difficulties of the country. The volume of water in the Ganges Canal is here very large, and the controlling agencies are in proportion: at one point, a massive aqueduct spans a large river; at another, a river, mingling its waters with the canal, passes through it at right angles. At these places the regulating works are very extensive; any imperfection or carelessness would at times flood the canal throughout its course, and cause incalculable damage by submerging a large extent of country. The Ganges Canal, being as yet almost destitute of trees on its banks, looks really like a canal in all respects;

but the scenery surrounding this portion of it is improved by the vicinity of mountains, particularly at this season of the year, when the wild storms of the monsoon were sweeping over the Himalaya heights, which were just distant enough to impress us with their full height and grandeur.

As the evening advanced, we saw heavy storms descending encircle in their embrace the Sawaliks, or lower ranges of the Himalayas, in which the smaller rivers take their rise; and the low, distant rumbling of the thunder amongst their rugged ravines led us to anticipate that a "row," or mountain torrent in flood, might inconvenience us, as we should be compelled to cross some of the many streams of this kind which intercepted our course. These torrents are carried over the canal on arches, forming a bridge or aqueduct; but, curious to say, they are themselves not bridged, and on this account must at times prove a great inconvenience to the canal authorities. Two or three miles from Jwallapore, we found our anticipations verified, and it was some time before we could make up our minds to cross the torrent before us. However, abandoning our dog-cart, we took off part of our clothes, and reached the opposite side none the worse for the timber and stones rolling down the stream; but our precautions to save our clothes from becoming wet, by placing them on our heads, did not succeed. We walked into Jwallapore, where we found that the tents and baggage, having been pulled up, in consequence of the same "row" a little higher up the stream, had not appeared; so that a rather uncomfortable night's sleep in wet clothes was the result. The discomfort, however, was of slight moment, as such an event had become to all of us a common occurrence. It was the probability, almost amounting to a certainty, of fever supervening upon this sort of exposure, which caused us some anxiety. Such a result would necessarily lead to the sacrifice of this portion of the district, as every day's delay would render the low, swampy jungle we were entering more unhealthy and more impenetrable to Europeans. The success of all our plans depended on keeping in tolerable health and being able to stick to our saddles.

The rain during the 14th of July having delayed the arrival of a certain portion of our armament, a halt at Jwallapore became necessary. The arrangement regarding the Raos' contingent, some 150 men, to be furnished on the morrow, was completed at an early hour. Having nothing better to engage our time, and thinking the apparent contempt it would show for the present state of affairs might exercise a salutary influence on our friends, Captain D——d and myself started with our guns and a few elephants to beat up some game in the neighbourhood. On our return, an Affghan friend of the Raos, detained here by the state of the country, referring to the existing disturbances, remarked that, on our arrival, he expected to find the Englishmen care-worn and anxious; but this he had not found the case, and he had heard that those in charge of districts throughout the country had enrolled themselves as troopers, and were risking their lives as much as, or more so than, the commonest soldier. This fact seemed to have made a strong impression on his mind, and augured well, he thought, as to our ultimate prospects.

From subsequent conversations with natives in various parts of the country, it appeared that nothing had astonished them all so much as the rapidity with which Englishmen of every class at once sprang to arms. They had long looked on the magistrates and collectors, planters, &c., as being by nature and habit as thoroughly separated by caste from English soldiers as their own bunyahs and kayuths. It was, moreover, contrary to all native ideas of propriety that those entrusted with administrative powers, which they consider the highest, should demean themselves with soldiering. Their own history is a tissue of records, in which intrigue, sitting aloof from all danger, has gained victories and conquered countries. Even the battle of Plassy, won by Englishmen, shows that we did not then despise fighting them with their own weapons. Natives do not understand a good stand-up fight, incurring considerable loss to the victors; but they appreciate intrigue, converting a foe into a friend in the hour of battle, followed by an instantaneous rout and prodigious slaughter, but the slaughter must be of an unresisting enemy, or, if possible, and preferable, because accompanied with less danger, an unresisting peasantry, or the effeminate residents of a city. Such a victory would be something worth talking about for the next twenty generations.

Hindustanis invariably have recourse to intrigue, considering it superior in its results to hard knocks and generalship. If it were possible at all to drive this out of their heads, the late rebellion ought to have that effect, but so vain is the race, that, confidence being restored, many a man would be found ready to affirm, in simple honesty, that, considering themselves cleverer by far than the English, the time will come when they will yet intrigue them out of the country. Driving them out would never enter into the same sage noodle's brain, who is coward, every inch of him; the only men who dream of the time—and they do so constantly—when the English are to be driven out of the country are the Pathans, Ranghurs, and other Mahomedans.

We started at daybreak on the 15th of July, with the intention of attacking Futtuah, if possible, the same day, and then encamping near it. A friend and myself went in advance with our cavalry, but no enemy was to be seen. Our track lay through an undulating country, at first only partially covered with jungle. From the cleared portions of land many old forest trees had not been removed, and their solitary grandeur formed a pleasing relief; but it was melancholy to look on the blackened ruins of burned villages here and there, now totally deserted. Not a vestige of life was there to represent the villages that I had but a few months earlier noticed in apparently comfortable circumstances, beyond, perhaps, an emaciated dog or cat, which only served to cast a darker shade over the desolation of the abodes. The whole scene was more completely that of desolation than I had yet noticed elsewhere, as a result of the rebellion; it brought vividly before one's imagination the native accounts of the extermination accompanying the inroads of the Goorkhas of old.

We wandered on admiring the rich and lovely tract of country, recognizing now and then the frequent large mounds indicating the ruins of ancient towns. This had, some two hundred years previously, been a densely peopled and rich locality, but the Goorkhas were then carrying everything before them, wresting province after province from the effeminate successors of the Mahomedan conquerors of Hindustan; this eastern portion of the Saharunpore district became in its turn one of their conquests. With true Indo-Chinese ferocity, every male was put to the sword by the Goorkhas, and the women carried off as slaves to the interior of their hills. All became a wilderness, and has only of late been slowly recovering under the British rule. One swoop of these

Bunjarahs had now driven off the scanty population of the few villages which have for years been nursed on the government grants, and were only just struggling into healthy vitality, the climate at present being sadly against them. Though the tract of country between Jwallapore and Futtuah is generally slightly elevated, it is surrounded by extensive swampy jungles, and all who can afford it, even in times of peace, abandon the place during the rains. As population increases, and the jungle is cleared to the extent reported to have been the case in former days, this great unhealthiness will in some measure disappear, though by no means altogether, as much land is constantly flooded by the Ganges, Solani, and other streams, and the whole is intersected by vast swamps, which deer, pigs, tigers, and wild elephants alone haunt with impunity during the monsoon.

Never having been here during the rains, I was much struck with the luxuriance and beauty of the vegetation; nor was the charm diminished by the proximity of those glorious footprints of the Creator, the snowy ranges of the Himalayas, which so vividly impress upon all the sublimity of their great Source. The overpowering abundance, however, of insect life, and vicious, ever-pursuing horse-flies of a peculiarly poisonous kind, at times unmistakably impressed on us, in the stillness of these woodland solitudes, the unhealthiness of the locality. We rode on very pleasantly until arriving under Ranee Majra, a deserted village, surrounded by dense jungle, which had already overgrown many of the ruined houses. Here we were confronted by a flooded river, called the Bangunga, as, indeed, we partly anticipated, though we did not expect the river to turn out unfordable. As, however, we could not control its fancies, we encamped round the unfortunate village, after reconnoitring parties had ascertained that the Bunjarahs had all crossed to the left bank of the stream.

On the following day, the 16th of July, some boats which had been sent for from the Ganges Canal arrived; but the Bangunga rose still higher, covering all the low lands for miles, the whole country presenting one vast sheet of troubled waters. This would not of itself have prevented our crossing, but the fall of the Bangunga was rapid. Being close to the hills, which are here invariably covered with timber, its whole course was obstructed by large trees torn up from the roots; the roots and branches at times alternately darting high out of the water, as they met with opposition from below in their reckless course. Any of this timber striking a boat would have destroyed it at once; we were obliged, therefore, to remain in our present encamping ground.

While at breakfast, we heard firing, which, considering the state of the country, we hardly expected; and shortly after, information arrived that some of our camp followers had been attacked by the Bunjarahs. While the troops were getting under arms, Captain D——d and myself wandered in the direction of the firing, to see into the state of affairs, and were shortly fired at by a body of men in the jungle. The Bunjarahs are accustomed to kill tigers and other wild animals with their matchlocks; they were consequently good shots, and should have been formidable in jungle warfare; but they did not prove so, probably from the want of good leaders. Taking advantage of the cover ourselves, we soon made our opponents feel the superiority of English rifles, and speedily obliged them to abandon their advanced position. When our little army arrived, but few of the enemy could be seen, though, doubtless, numbers were concealed in the surrounding jungle, into which a discharge or two of grape being sent, we saw no more of the gentlemen.

On the 17th, the river fell considerably, and we commenced crossing, an operation which occupied us some four hours. The Raos' contingent had now been with us two days; a large proportion of them were really well armed, some with English double-barrelled guns. Their armament rather took me aback; I expected a miserable rabble, and the requisition had been made only with the view of rendering our force in the field numerically larger, by being able to leave these men with the camp, or sending them to procure information; but, being, contrary to all expectation, well armed, and so completely outnumbering us, their very efficiency rendered them by no means pleasant allies in the present state of affairs, as they would have met with no difficulty in coming to terms with the Bunjarahs. At first they were civil enough; but our numerical weakness soon induced contempt, which latterly they did not disguise, causing some inconvenience and anxiety, from the impossibility of leaving them in charge of our camp.

We began crossing the Bangunga early in the morning. While Captain M——n, with the sappers and the gun, passed over the stream, which was still broad and rapid, it was my lot to remain behind with part of the Putteeala Horse, looking on at operations in general. At last all was ready for my party to move forward, and we were waiting for the boat, when a party of the Raos' men assembled near me, talking loudly and with marked insolence, in that demonstrative manner so peculiar to the Hindustani. The boat came alongside the bank, when one of the leading men under the Raos walked up as if to step on board before me, this in itself being a pointed mark of disrespect, which he improved upon by forcing his way so rudely that he nearly pushed me down the slippery bank. This was a little too much. After a second's reflection, my determination was taken, and, knocking the man down, my rifle was instantly ready for resistance from the others. But they were Hindustanis. The man himself skulked back among his comrades, who soon looked quite pleased, and we all crossed over the best of friends. These men subsequently behaved well, and with extreme respect, but this did not disarm our suspicions. On the first excuse, that of escorting recovered cattle, they were sent back to Jwallapore, and, on departing, they received the full quota of Hindustani compliments for their assistance and usefulness, as their good-will was still necessary: if inclined, they had it in their power to interrupt our communications, as Jwallapore had become our actual base of operations.

After crossing the river, a wounded Bunjarah was discovered in the tree jungle amongst some long grass. This man must have been accidentally forgotten by his companions when retreating, as he had evidently been carried to his present position, and it was a wonder that no wild animals had got hold of him during the night. He was an intelligent, handsome young man. A rifle-ball, the wound caused by which we could at first hardly discover, had broken his leg near the thigh, so that he was unable to move, and in considerable pain; he was much relieved when Captain D——d bound up the leg with strips of bark torn from a neighbouring tree. This man reported that a larger number had been killed and wounded on the previous day than we had any idea of, and amongst others, the two relations of Sherah, their leader.

We now advanced through the forest and long grass jungle without meeting any opposition, in a country, too, where a few good marksmen might have done infinite mischief. On approaching the Ganges, we came upon some cleared tracts surrounding a few small villages, and thence skirting the river, arrived at Futtuah, the head-quarters of the Bunjarahs, who, we found, had abandoned the place with a considerable portion of its stores of plundered corn, and had taken refuge on a rather large island in the Ganges, the stream of which at this season more resembles a large lake, though it flows with extreme rapidity. Some part of the store of corn and cattle, and much of the Bunjarahs' own property, was carried away or driven off by the Jwallapore Raos' party, and the rapidity with which these men discovered herds of cattle secreted in the jungle was very satisfactory. As all the boats on the Ganges had been removed or destroyed, it was found impossible to pursue the Bunjarahs into their swampy islands; so, beyond giving them a discharge or two of grape, we left them alone. They, however, evidently felt the loss of their cattle severely, and seeing that rebellion was a losing game, they shortly after sued for terms, by proposing to deliver up their leaders. We now returned again, *viâ* Jwallapore, to Roorkie, all glad to escape from this vast swamp.

CHAPTER IX.

Another rising round Deobund—March thither—Results of the rebel attack on Deobund—Manliness of the low castes—Anecdote of the capture of a Brahmun boy by the Rajpoots—His recovery—Tradition, and its results in the rebellion—Hindoo houses—Hurried return to Saharunpore—The Bijnour rebels, and progress of the siege of Delhi—Danger to be apprehended from the Seikhs—The Khazee of Thanah Bhawun—Massacre of the government officials there—Reverses at Thanah Bhawun—Rebels evacuate the place on the advance of a second force—March to Rampore— Seikhs summoned from Jugaduree—A lady's trip to Umballah—Encamp at Rampore—Disappearance of the rebels—Return to Saharunpore, and march to the north—The Eastern Jumna Canal—Affghan appreciation of the beautiful in nature—Padshah Mahal; anecdote of its abandonment—Raipore—Implicated parties surrender themselves, and are released—Return to Saharunpore—Departure for the banks of the Ganges—Effect of the fall of Delhi on the native mind—Agreeable change in our position—Missionary zeal—Gratitude of the moneyed classes for British protection—District duties at an end.

Shortly after the preceding events at Roorkie, I arrived and received information that the whole country round Deobund had again risen with the intention of attacking that important place. With nearly the same heterogeneous force employed in the Khâdir of the Ganges, we at once proceeded in that direction; and two days' march, during which we visited some rebel villages in the Mozuffurnugur district, brought us to the vicinity of the city, in approaching which place we intercepted several bands of men returning to their homes with the plunder of Deobund; for the attacking parties, having timely notice of our advance, scattered to their homes on our approach. The same scenes that had occurred at Nookur had here been re-enacted on a larger scale; the attack having originated from nearly the same motives, viz., plunder and the destruction of bunyahs' accounts and bonds. In Deobund, however, the resistance on the part of the townspeople had been more determined, the enemy more numerous, and the loss of life on both sides very considerable. I ought to remark that the valour of the citizens had consisted in hiring for battle, at high rates of remuneration, the Bhungies and other low castes, whom in ordinary times they despised, compelling them to live on the outskirts of the town, so as not to defile its pure inhabitants. The moneyed classes (bunyahs and mahajuns) did not seem to have ever personally attempted resistance, though many of them were killed or wounded after their more manly low-caste retainers were overpowered.

On my arrival, these valiant moneyed classes hoped to awaken my sympathy by showing me their wounds; but they aroused only disgust for their cowardice, their wounds being almost invariably on the back. The hired Bhungies, however, who were numerically much inferior to their Rajpoot and Goojur assailants, fought bravely, inflicting a much severer loss than they suffered, as the corpses of the latter, piled up in a heap outside the city, clearly proved. Several days were now spent in the neighbourhood of Deobund, and many of the most notorious villages in the neighbourhood punished. Two days were employed in bringing forward for recognition and trial some of the most deeply implicated of our prisoners. A further advance, however, into the Khatah, which had been most unfortunately delayed on account of the unceasing rain and flooded state of the country, was again put off indefinitely on account of requisitions from the station of Saharunpore. The only course open to us was to deal severely with the most notorious of our prisoners, with the hope of overawing the Khatah Rajpoots, and fortunately our policy had the anticipated effect, as we were not again seriously troubled by these men.

During the attack on Deobund, certain Rajpoots managed to lay their hands on the son of a wealthy inhabitant of the place, whom they removed and secreted with the view of extorting a ransom. It was an object, if possible, to recover this boy, if merely to demonstrate the vitality of our power, but his whereabouts was by no means easily ascertained. On investigation it turned out that the villagers who had first captured him were attacked by a party from another village, who considered that a share of the anticipated ransom money fairly belonged to them, having been co-parceners in the attack on Deobund. The result of the encounter was, that the captive changed hands; but the ill-will resulting from this affray enabled me to ascertain exactly where the boy was concealed.

Early one morning before sunrise, after a rather perplexing march across country in the dark, the village where he was kept prisoner was surrounded, and this being done, the offer of a hundred rupees to any trooper who would bring the child out alive had the desired effect. The boy was in our possession before the majority of the people in the village were awake. Instead of gratitude on the part of the rich old vagabond who had expressed such deep anxiety on account of the child, we afterwards found it very difficult to extract from him the paltry reward of a hundred rupees, though the enterprise was of such a nature that he had doubted the policy of attempting to rescue the boy, from the likelihood of his being killed should we attack the parties in whose possession he was. The manner in which the Rajpoots removed this Brahmun boy to secure a ransom is one instance illustrative of the rapidity with which natives, throughout this revolt, at once reverted to the pursuits of their forefathers.

Tradition never loses its charm amongst Hindustanis. Natives universally remarked to me that one half of the risings amongst the rural population might be attributed to the traditions existing among the Rajpoots and other warlike races, of the manner in which their forefathers used to swagger about the country well armed, and obtain a livelihood by plundering the less warlike. These were the days of the Rajpoot supremacy; and they considered that, by a happy turn of events, those glorious times had at last returned again. They accordingly entered into the sport with a hearty good-will, though, after a while, finding that the loss more than counterbalanced the gain, they became thoroughly sick of anarchy, and longed again for repose. Hence, the rapidity with which they at once settled down to their peaceful avocations, as if nothing had ever taken place, whenever our columns marched through our older provinces.

When searching some of the wealthier inhabitants' houses in Deobund, I was struck by the invariable novelty of several small rooms perched on the top of the flat roofs, but so placed as not to be easily seen from the streets, or from the tops of neighbouring houses. In many of these rooms, chairs were swung between the door-jambs. On inquiring, I found that during the rains, the ladies of the household are fond of reclining in these chairs, which are kept swinging by a rope attached to the back. For hours they thus listlessly amuse themselves, listening to all the scandal of the day collected by their female attendants. It seems they are particularly fond of this pastime when the rain is falling, which, every now and then, wets them slightly. Much trouble as I had long previously taken to ascertain the habits of the people, these sudden visits among the better class of houses during the disturbances, disclosed many curious features never brought under my observation, even in the extensive disclosures from time to time made public in an Indian magistrate's court. The antiquated simplicity which characterises many of their domestic arrangements recalls the days of Sacountalla; but the illusion fades on beholding some vile French picture, introduced with the advance of European civilization. Still, these large houses, with their fifty or so very small rooms, without the least attempt at ventilation, and with scarcely space to turn in, must be anything but comfortable or healthy during the hot season. The numerous apartments were probably designed for the secretion of valuable property, the contrivances for securing which are very ingenious, and would with difficulty be discovered by a European without native assistance.

While in the neighbourhood of Deobund, an old schoolfellow of mine, having escaped with his wife from Moradabad, had written to me from Mozuffurnugur, some twenty-five miles distant, to inquire if I could furnish him with an escort to Saharunpore, as, in consequence of sickness, it was necessary for him to proceed, if possible, to the Himalayas. My answer was, that if he came within a certain time, he should have the escort. This period had elapsed, and was considerably lengthened, yet no one appeared; and, as ample time had been given, I supposed my friend's plans had been changed. On the other hand, our return to Saharunpore was imperative; that place, we had reason to believe, being threatened by the enemy. How great was my surprise, on arriving at the station, to find that my friend and his wife had arrived before me. Our march had, doubtless, for a time, scattered the rebels to a considerable distance from the neighbourhood of the road, yet this portion of the country was swarming with parties that would only have been too glad to cut off any straggling Europeans, and all the better fun from a lady forming one of the party. It turned out that on nearing Deobund, where my friend still expected to find me, the palkee-bearers—whether in accordance with custom, from which natives never willingly depart, I know not—took their charge in the direction of, and deposited them close to, the ruins of the staging bungalow amongst a clump of fine trees. Here, instead of supposed friends, these two were greeted by the bodies of men hanging on the surrounding trees; enough in quiet times, in a lonely spot, and late in the evening, to affect seriously stronger nerves than those of a young lady, whose previous experience had probably been chiefly confined to a London drawing-room. These trees, being near the high-road, and close to the staging bungalow burnt by the rebels, had been selected by me as a fitting locality for the execution of the rebels condemned on the previous days, and their bodies were purposely left hanging on the spot as a warning and menace, it being impossible for us to remain in the neighbourhood and maintain order, while it was absolutely necessary that quiet should be restored, even at the cost of the severest measures, or our communications with the south would again be closed.

On the arrival of my friend at this locality, finding that I had vanished, he determined to go on at once —a fortunate resolve, as in a few hours the road would have been closed to such helpless travellers. It was fortunate, too, that night was approaching, when natives rarely wander about if they can possibly avoid doing so. The courage and energy of this young lady—by no means accustomed to rough it, risking all cheerfully to secure a healthy change for her husband—struck all of us as one of many similar instances during the rebellion, which made Englishmen proud of their race, and united them closer in mutual respect.

As the rains had for some time been very heavy, and the whole country was under water, we gladly turned our faces towards Saharunpore, especially as some of our party were suffering from illness. Indeed, all the more important portions of the district had now in turns been visited by me, and received substantial warnings, while the season of the year had become even more unfavourable to natives than to Europeans. It was consequently hardly a matter of surprise that, with but slight interruptions, the district remained reasonably quiet till the fall of Delhi. My superior, falling ill about that time, left for the hills, the charge of the district devolving upon me.

But while the district remained quiet, the Bijnour rebels, on the left bank of the Ganges, were assuming a more organized form, and a descent might be expected at any moment, while the progress of our arms at Delhi was becoming a more anxious subject than it had ever been. We felt that the long-looked-for assault must be pressed on at every reasonable risk. All knew that the Seikhs were in a dangerous state. Were Delhi ours, all was ours. The joyous news at last came, and though every demonstration in the way of firing salutes, parading our force, &c., was made to convince those around us that that event had actually taken place, for a long time the people did not believe in it, and many infatuated individuals had unfortunately selected this inauspicious moment to join in the rebellion.

The Khazee of Thanah Bhawun, a place in the Mozuffurnugur district, and on the southern borders of our own, after murdering all the native officials of that place under circumstances of peculiar atrocity and treachery, had unfortunately succeeded in driving off a small party of Goorkhas and other troops, who had not been well managed when attacking him.

This made matters serious, as any slight defeat at that time ordinarily induced a general rising. A considerable force was consequently at once marched out from Meeruth to attack Thanah Bhawun. The place was abandoned, as usual, by the rebels on seeing that the force opposed to them was more than their match, and they entered our district in considerable numbers, which necessitated my leaving Saharunpore rather hurriedly, to intercept them with some Seikh military mounted police under a native commandant.

In consequence of all the men that could be parted with having been sent to assist the Mozuffurnugur force, we had hardly enough Goorkhas remaining to guard even the gaol and treasury. In the absence of the military police, the rebels might double behind me and attack the station; I therefore summoned some Seikhs of the Ferozepore and Loodiana regiments, under a European officer, stationed at Jugaduree, on the right bank of the Jumna in the Umballah district, which force had been placed at my disposal by the Commissioner of Umballah. As some ladies had insisted on coming to Saharunpore from the Himalayas, under the impression that it was safer than the latter place, I left with the Seikh military police, without informing any one, so as not to create alarm. The noise of the horses, however, attracted the attention of the more wakeful. One lady who had escaped with her children from Delhi, after her husband had been murdered, became so alarmed on this discovery that she left at once for Umballah, with her children, in a palkee. Had the Seikhs summoned from that direction not been accidentally on the road, the consequences might have been serious to her, it being impossible to calculate which direction the rebels might take; moreover, the country she traversed had not long since been in open rebellion, which, under any circumstances, rendered the trip not over-secure to parties unable to defend themselves. She arrived, however, quite safely at Umballah.

Near the end of our march and about midnight, when approaching the ground where the rebels might be expected, the native gentleman commanding the Seikh horse stated that he could not answer for his men fighting; they had, he said, been hurriedly raised for police purposes, and not intended for this kind of work. This information was rather late in the day, so, abandoning all intention of attacking that night, we advanced a few miles, and encamped near the town of Rampore. The news of the advent, as I anticipated, of a body of Seikhs, number and quality unknown, was rapidly spread abroad, and before morning the rebels had decamped. For the sake of the moral effect expected from their presence, this force, under their native commandant, was left in the neighbourhood for a few days; and, having been useful in their way, they were shortly after returned to the Punjaub. The authorities there, in the meantime, having been good enough to sanction the retention of the Ferozepore Seikhs and of a portion of the 1st Punjaub Cavalry, these troops were strength sufficient for our requirements, but not more than sufficient, as the Ganges was rapidly falling, and the Bijnour rebels threatened to invade our district.

A considerable portion of our force had been sent out to watch the Ganges frontier, when an unexpected gathering took place in our own district, in the neighbourhood of Kulseea; which caused me to proceed there with 200 Seikhs under a European officer, and 50 horse with their Affghan russaldar. Kulseea was towards the source of the Eastern Jumna Canal, and I was always delighted when duty called me in this direction. This canal was formed by Murdan Khan, the favourite and wealthy minister of Shah Jehan, Emperor of Delhi. Like all native constructions of the kind, levels had been defectively taken; but, unlike our more scientific but less picturesque canals, its wandering course much resembles a river, and the fall not being well regulated, the stream is at times very rapid, at others still and deep. Being imbedded in trees and surrounded by mountains in this locality, it possesses every requisite of a beautiful river. Wandering along its banks on approaching the hills, with views of the snowy ranges peeping through the deep, tropical foliage veiling the cold crystal stream below, the scene is enchanting, and one for a time forgets the burning sun of India, not the less fatal because in sight of snow.

The rough Affghans accompanying us seemed fully to appreciate these beautiful landscapes, and delighted to compare them with their own mountain valleys; for, unlike the Hindustanis, they are keenly sensitive to the beautiful in nature. Hindustanis understand a beautiful shawl, pipe, or other ornamental production that they consider costly; but though so extraordinarily sensitive and subtle in trifles, to a casual observer almost implying an educated and refined organization, they neither understand nor appreciate beauties which are the creation of a higher nature than theirs, and which tell of Almighty power.

Close to Khara, and near the point where the canal receives its supply of water from the Jumna, are situated the ruins of a palace, called Padshah Mahal, "the king's abode," built by Murdan Khan for his master, Shah Jehan. In the selection of this beautiful site for the palace, Murdan Khan's Affghan descent, with its love of nature, is unmistakably evinced. Situated on rather a high point, overhanging the Jumna, the windows of this palace command some lovely views. To the south is stretched out Hindustan, with the various rivers meandering in broad, silvery tracings over its boundless plains, while to the north the eye follows the clear, rapid waters of the Jumna into the rugged labyrinth of the Himalayas. In my opinion, the scene is, on the whole, finer than at Hurdwar on the Ganges, as the river there is more rapidly hidden amongst the mountains. In this entrancing spot, Shah Jehan, after all, made but a brief sojourn. As usual in Oriental States, oppression attended the footsteps of the monarch, and the surrounding zemindars set their wits to work to get rid of their royal visitor. They wisely determined to effect this through the Emperor's zanana; for though thus confined, in no country do women possess greater power, or more frequently become political celebrities, than in India. In the neighbouring mountains, goitre is a very common disease; so the zemindars collected from thence all the goitred women they could get hold of, and daily despatched them into the zanana with presents of fruit, &c. The universality of the goitre soon attracted the attention of the ladies, and to every inquiry the affected replied that none ever lived any length of time in the locality without being afflicted with this disease. As a natural result, Shah Jehan got no peace from the ladies of his household till Padshah Mahal was abandoned for ever.

On arriving at our destination, Raipore, the implicated parties thought fit to deliver themselves up, and I shortly after released them, as a reward for their good behaviour during more critical times, when from their influence they might have seriously complicated our position. When I returned to Saharunpore, leaving that town in charge of the assistant magistrate, I again left for the banks of the Ganges, where existed the only prominent enemy left. But now the work was of a princely stamp, when contrasted with the early days of the revolt. There were some half-dozen officers to do the soldiering, nor was I now associated with troops who might shoot me at any moment. We had a constant recurrence of small encounters, and on one or two occasions the enemy managed to plan their attacks with sufficient precision, to surprise and scatter our advance picquets on the banks of the Ganges; but, on the whole, with the cold season rapidly advancing, and the cautious Bijnour rebels, though now reinforced and tolerably well appointed, hardly likely to cross in force, so as to place a large river to their rear, our duties became a pleasant relaxation, in the absence of that killing anxiety of former days. It is a satisfaction, moreover, to feel that the tide of fortune has decidedly turned, and yourself at last actually on the winning side, after so much protracted uncertainty and suspense. Those distant from the scene of action can hardly appreciate the invigorating sensation that imparted a new life to Europeans in northern India, when our small columns moved out to conquer after the fall of Delhi, with no withering incubus of a Crimean hero to retard their movements.

Early in the disturbances, it being evident that the outbreak had assumed a religious character, the missionaries at Saharunpore had been requested to proceed to the hills. Immediately after the fall of Delhi, a junior member of this mission, with more zeal than discretion, returned and announced his intention of preaching in public in the city. Saharunpore is essentially a Mahomedan city, and at no time possessed the reputation of being deficient in turbulence. When this young man made his appearance, the natives still disbelieved in the fall of Delhi, and our reverses, so close as Thanah Bhawun, were the general theme of conversation. This missionary understood Hindustani very imperfectly, and unintentionally might have perpetrated some horrible blunder, which, though only exciting laughter in ordinary times, would at that time have roused all the dormant animosity of his hearers; so that, on attempting to preach, he would, in all likelihood, have been himself killed, and even provoked a Mahomedan rising as the ultimate result. I sent for the gentleman and remonstrated, but he departed, obstinately insisting that it was his duty. Not until informed by a friend that, on attempting anything of the kind, he would be seized by the police, and deported out of the district in the company of a couple of troopers, did he give in. This extent of indiscreet zeal amongst missionaries in northern India is very rare indeed; and it was the more extraordinary as evinced by a member of the American missions, who are such thoroughly practical, sincere men, and the only missionaries that seem at all successful in conquering the deep caste prejudices of the North-West Provinces. In justice, however, it should be mentioned that this gentleman's superiors, not then present, much deprecated the mistaken zeal of their subordinate, in which light he himself now doubtless views it.

As an illustration of the gratitude and friendship of the moneyed classes in India, who owe their all to the British Government, the following instance is given, as it occurred about this time:—In the month of October, 1857, when sadly pressed by the deficiency of means to enable me to meet the necessary disbursements of the district, I called on the Saharunpore mahajuns, or bankers, to furnish me with by no means a heavy loan. This they positively refused to do, declaring their inability to meet my wishes; that is, to that Government who has never imposed any description of tax upon this class (a great oversight, by the way), and through whose protection alone they had been enabled to accumulate their wealth, these men refused a portion of that capital which would have disappeared with the Government which had fostered them. At such a juncture, indeed, their refusal would have been of little moment; for had I not almost immediately received an unexpected supply from other quarters, these vermin might have learnt that necessity is sometimes superior to laws, and that we had not protected their property at the risk of our lives without expecting some reasonable return, should circumstances render it necessary. But never will Indian bankers, if they can avoid it, lend money to the State, as they somewhat justly argue that the Government, on seeing their wealth, might at last open its eyes, and suggest some trifle towards the expense of defending their vast accumulations.

On being relieved of my district duties, I shortly after entered on my new avocation as a member of the commission for the trial of mutineers and rebels, which necessitated my joining various field forces to the south of Saharunpore, and I ultimately found myself in Sir Colin Campbell's encampment at Futtehgurh. I hardly need say that it was indeed a relief to take refuge at last under the wing of a European army such as India had never before seen, little troubled by shot or shell, and without a thought for the morrow, or as to the state of one's arms; nor is it very necessary to add, that long companionship with, and dependence on, the Hindustanis had far from endeared their society to me.

CHAPTER X.

Importance in India of a well-considered system of fortifications and fortified outposts—Their great advantages on the recurrence of any crisis—Note on the services of the civilians in India —Hindustani *versus* English atrocities—Extremes of public opinion and responsibility of the press—The exaggerated stories of the Eurasians considered—Letter to the *Times* from Lucknow—Certain facts beyond contradiction—Reasons for the deficiency of actual evidence—Native character, and the treatment it demands—India visited by members of Parliament and others—Evil consequences of the accusations against the English in India.

So long as England is not hard pressed by a European war at home, and maintains the mastery of the seas, the high metal of her race will doubtless carry everything before it in India; and this, too, in spite of embarrassments occasioned by parliamentary action on events passing six or eight thousand miles distant, in a country where the whole aspect of affairs may have changed even while these wonderful conclusions are being formed. Since the change in the Indian home administration, whatever may be the results of these parliamentary squabbles or changes of ministry, one thing, at any rate, is certain, that in India, unless Englishmen take full advantage of the warnings offered by this revolt, the succeeding generation may witness another rising of even a more serious character.

Englishmen, depending, it would seem, on their wooden walls, have learnt to reflect but little on the importance of securing their frail tenure of this vast country by the ordinary precaution of fortified posts. A few forts, it is true, were commenced, while hostilities lasted and immediate danger threatened; also, some old constructions were partially placed in repair; but the supply is hardly sufficient. The existence of forts where military munitions and treasure can be securely stored, enables the majority of a station force to move out for aggressive purposes, or join any army in the field; and if, in addition, a well-considered system of railways connected these forts, we should more than quadruple the working strength of our small European army.

Forts, however, are not the only fortifications required. This rebellion has demonstrated clearly enough that, let the civil officers in charge of districts show the least inclination to abandon their head-quarters, and British authority at once ceases to exist in a tract of country as large as half a dozen or more English counties; and that, in such case, a trifling disturbance assumes at once the proportions of a rebellion. To obviate a too early, and perhaps unnecessary retreat, when a crisis occurs, every out-district in India should possess a fortified house for the security of the treasure. This house should not be too large, but capable of being held by from ten to thirty Europeans for a couple of weeks, or till the arrival of relief.

I know several districts in the North-West Provinces where the treasure and records would have been saved during the last revolt, and, perhaps, even the district itself, had such a house existed. Even if not attacked or obliged to stand a siege, its very existence would induce civilians (if not better advised by past experience*) to remain longer at their posts when rebellion was closing in around them; while the mere presence of Europeans in charge of the districts would, in all probability, as we have frequently seen during this revolt, keep the more powerful and far-sighted of the natives on the side of the British Government and order. In short, these fortified houses, though untenable against a force accompanied by artillery, would form a strong bulwark against revolt, and not a man who has passed through this rebellion but has seen the absoute necessity of some such provision. I am aware of the difficulty that some may feel, wanting a superfluity of cash for such purposes; but the construction

* A third of the civilians present in the North-West Provinces and Oude during the late revolt forfeited their lives in their chivalrous devotion to their duty, or, in other words, a larger proportion were killed than in any branch of the army in those provinces, and the services of the entire body have been simply ignored by the home Government. The hint may perhaps be taken.

of these simple works might easily be carried out by convicts, at a very slight expense to the State.

And here I may remark that, whatever precautions are taken to secure our position in India, it will at any rate ensure the maximum of contempt from the natives (and the next step to contempt is revolt), if we endeavour to impress them with the conviction that we wilfully closed our eyes to much of the iniquity of which they were the authors during the late revolt; and that, after all, the most influential of the English race are not merely their apologists, but are ready to maintain that Hindustanis are, on the whole, superior to their conquerors. In this particular the press has much to answer for. Though the greater number of Europeans in India, not being creatures of a parliamentary majority, have little respect in general for the expression of English public opinion in regard to Indian affairs, there can be no doubt that more harm than good has accrued from ill-natured criticisms; for even now the violent and unreasonable changes which have succeeded one another on the subject of Hindustani *versus* English atrocities, have apparently settled down into anything but correct conclusions.

In 1857, during the desperate struggle for English supremacy in the North-West Provinces, in the early stages of the revolt, English public opinion, as represented by its press, astonished by the violence of its denunciations even actors amidst scenes of revolt and bloodshed; but hardly had the news of returning success reached England, and it had become evident that the men by whose prompt energy the crisis of the rebellion had been overcome were carrying everything before them, than no abuse seemed sufficiently severe to hurl at these astonished gentlemen, as a reward for their efforts in supporting their country's interests at great personal risk. This uncalled-for excitement increased even to a greater degree when some unfortunate Eurasians, not yet recovered from the effects of the scenes through which they had passed (and it must be remembered many of the poorer amongst them are hardly above the level of the humbler classes of the natives), falling into the hands of illiterate men, anxious to make out a good story, produced, with the assistance of the latter, evidently exaggerated statements of their sufferings at the hands of the natives. Though exaggerated, however, and thus rendered a little incredible, these statements possessed only too deep and melancholy a tinge of truth.

The tales told by the poor Eurasians were in fact much nearer the real state of affairs than some assertions of an opposite import made by certain equally feeble-minded individuals. At first, horribly alarmed, but finding to their astonishment that they had actually done the mutinies in perfect security in the Punjaub, or down country, without ever having seen a rebel or mutineer, unless securely bound, or ever having been in a position to investigate the subject they were commenting on, these men came to the conclusion that all they had heard was false, and scribbled to the papers their ill-natured ideas before it had even come within the bounds of human possibility that the facts could be discovered.* The

* The most important of this class of statements was the production of a certain Mr. G—— C——, who writes to the *Times* from Lucknow on the 5th of June, 1858, that the stories of "dishonour, &c., are the purest inventions." And again, "As regards dishonour, I believe that the feeling towards our race was not that which leads to such acts. It is more like the rising of one form of creation against another, like demons attacking angels, and trying to hurl them down;" with other rubbish of this kind. Mr. C—— may fancy himself an angel, perhaps is one, but most high-caste Hindoos and Mahomedans, apart from their dread of his power, view the cow and pig eating Englishman as the most unclean of vermin, very much in the same light that the man-eating New Zealander was formerly regarded by ourselves. If ever, then, making a distinction of the kind, they would certainly consider themselves the angels, the English the demons; so that Mr. C—— might have been nearer the truth, had he represented, that being angels the natives objected to interfere with demons. Not being myself acquainted with Mr. C——, either privately or in his official capacity, it seemed proper to make inquiries as to the means he possessed for ascertaining the truth, and the result was as follows: —On the outbreak of the mutiny, Mr. C—— retired to Simla, and on the supposed mutiny of the Nusseerees, descended to the Punjaub, where he resided till the fall of Delhi. Subsequently he advanced down country under the wing of Colonel Greathed's column, from the neighbourhood of which all natives, loyal or rebels, naturally vanished. This was succeeded by a trip to Calcutta, in expectancy of an appointment, with eventual success; and finally by his appearance at Lucknow to fill the appointment, and his letter thence to the *Times*. At the date of this last event (June 5th, 1858), investigations had, as yet, hardly commenced, while a large portion of the country was not even in our possession. Mr. C——'s friends were probably very glad to hear that he was actually in the land of the living; and a natural wish to lull their anxieties doubtless dictated the letter; but most reasoning

contradictory statements that had been published were doubtless confusing, but public opinion immediately flew to the opposite extreme, and not only declared all dishonour a fiction, but either denied the atrocities which had been committed, or wilfully attributed almost equal barbarity to the English themselves.

Perhaps the fickle tide of popular opinion has now turned sufficiently far to permit the murder of ladies and children, under circumstances hardly paralleled in history, to be considered atrocities in the worst sense, even though the whole of the facts attending those scenes may not yet have been disclosed to the public. Of the deliberate mutilation of Europeans, I came across no instances in my investigations; nor except in some cases where the parties are now living have I heard of such; but instances of mutilation and torture in the case of natives I met with constantly, where it had been practised in consequence of loyalty, supposed or real, to the British. Probably the fact that Englishmen almost invariably died fighting, was the chief reason why they escaped previous mutilation; still in the general confusion cases may have occurred of which all traces are obliterated, for "dead men tell no tales," and few Hindustanis are foolish enough to do so for them. As to dishonour, so far from its not taking place, my

beings would have seen that in a country only half conquered, and not yet subdued, time and patience alone would reveal the real facts, even if they could ever be satisfactorily sifted out amongst a population now bitterly hating us.

investigations firmly convinced me that it was as a general rule the case whenever the prisoners were not too emaciated by hardships to become objects of passion, as—it may be thought fortunately—was almost always the case with those of pure European extraction.

The localities, indeed, were few in which European ladies fell into the hands of the rebels, and those who did so were in general eventually exterminated, though evidence in some cases exists of their treatment. But all over the country there are a few scattered Eurasian women who were permitted to live after dishonour; and their account, or that of their husbands, is almost invariably the same. In judicial proceedings even these cases break down, in consequence of the impossibility of procuring a satisfactory recognition of the guilty parties from amongst the residents of a whole town or village; yet there cannot be a doubt as to the general truth of their assertions.

Further, in all these investigations, the investigators themselves are unwilling to inquire minutely, or dwell longer on such humiliating subjects; in cases, moreover, where the victims had been personal acquaintances or friends, and there appeared to be no hope of discovering the guilty parties, all proceedings were invariably quashed, as productive of no other result than pain to the relatives. If it were an object to ascertain the whole truth, it might be better effected two or three years hence, as race animosities gradually diminish; but enough has already been brought to light to satisfy all but the morbidly inquisitive. Except where the ends of justice are to be satisfied, a veil might well be dropped over so disagreeable a subject, which can only increase irritation on both sides, and be of no advantage to either party. There is a class of people, however, so impressed with the meek intelligence of the Hindoo race as in all respects superior to their own, that it would be impossible to convince them even by disclosing cases, the painful features of which all not so thoroughly kind-hearted shrink from. There were many, in fact too many, of this stamp,* even in India, who loved the sharp-witted Hindustani as dearly as they misunderstood his real character; but hardly had they overcome the alarm which followed the disappointment of their trust in the native character, and got alongside more manly spirits to show them the way, than it was found almost impossible to restrain their righteous indignation, and keep them from committing really cruel acts.

Though a master-analyst of character be necessary to define the mental and social peculiarities of a race with whose impulses and customs ours have

* It was a curious feature during the revolt that the servants of this class of Europeans almost always behaved treacherously or deserted their masters in the hour of danger, while those who treated their servants with firmness rarely repented it.

no affinity, still those weak peculiarities being better understood, beneficial results will alone be effected by at once acknowledging them. Looking the defects of the native in the face, resist or reform, but do not submit to them. By flattering or pampering the childish yet cruel follies of the Hindustani, pamperer and pampered invariably become disappointed, and end in hating each other. Let the native feel that you have measured his instincts, and he will at any rate respect you. As casually observed before, amongst other vagaries of English public opinion with reference to the revolt in India, has been the condemnation of their own countrymen for universal cruelty, founded on the supposition that, as one or two undeniable instances did exist on the evidence of some special newspaper correspondent or an erratic member of the House of Commons, consequently the whole English race in India were equally at fault. These horror-hunters, ignorant even of the language of the country, naturally commenced their journey under auspicious circumstances; and the latter throughout his trip was not only hoaxed into the most ridiculous conclusions, but, possessed of a lively enough discrimination, he reproduced these marvellous experiences in speeches to his gaping constituency on returning to England. Ordinarily in this world, particularly in judging mankind, one or two isolated cases, supposing these to be founded on truth, are hardly considered sufficient for sweeping condemnations. It might, for instance, by some at any rate, be thought that there was not much superfluity of sense in the composition of a foreigner who condemned a whole body of men in England, say the members of either of our houses of legislature, for deficiencies which had been manifested by individual members, and yet this is exactly what has occurred with reference to India. Are domesticated Englishmen so limited in their range of ideas as to suppose that all their countrymen, except some stray newspaper scribbler, change their natures in India, and are transformed into demons? No! it is your mild, domesticated gentleman, constantly dreaming of the horrors of French invasions, that is transformed into a demon when alarmed, though the placid calmness of his mind is something quite astounding when reviewing over a comfortable fire and glass of port-wine the cold-blooded murder of ladies and children, or the almost death-struggle of the surviving, these scenes being enacted at a most satisfactorily secure distance. Those, however, who crushed opposition in India, did so, fortunately, without much reference to the opinions prevailing amongst this class of their countrymen.

But these extravagant accusations have been productive of results probably little contemplated by the people or press originating them. When on the Continent, I observed, in conversation with foreigners, that the English, as a nation, are accused of the wildest cruelty, and convicted by the declamations of their own press. Foreigners, unfortunately, not understanding any fictitious distinctions between the English in India and England, have come to conclusions accordingly, and the character of the whole race has suffered in the estimation of other nations, for achieving which enviable notoriety England may thank enlightened press correspondents or equally sapient members of Parliament. If the Englishman himself did not previously understand some of the characteristics of his race, which apparently astonished him, but which led to the suppression of this rebellion in India, he can at any rate here discover that he is a most dangerous animal when brought to bay, though equally generous when victorious.

CHAPTER XI.

Connection between mutiny and rebellion in the North-West Provinces in 1857—Isolated instances of loyalty—Intestine wars—Necessity for unceasing caution—Vital importance of not mingling nationalities in the native regiments—Splitting up of the North-West Provinces into various nationalities during the revolt—Consequent want of co-operation and defeat of the rebel cause—Remarks on the rebel chiefs—Ancient boundaries of nationalities a subject of dispute—Rebel correspondence on this subject—Prospect of intestine wars had our power ceased—Universality of the last mutiny in consequence of nationalities not being defined in the Bengal army—The 10th Native Infantry—Antagonism between the Bhojpooreeas and Hindustanis—Rebel correspondence on the subject—Limits of the more important nationalities in the North-West Provinces defined—Composition of our native army—Dangerous character of the Puthan soldiery—Results during the revolt of indiscriminate recruiting in the Punjaub and Oude irregular forces—Remarks on the Goorkhas and Hindustanis—Mahomedans and Hindoos—High and low castes—Incident on Christmas day, 1858, near Sundee—Impossibility of ignoring caste prejudices—Universal falsification existing in the old native army—Precautions necessary to avoid the same in the new army—This falsification acting in favour of mutiny—Danger of making the Irregular Cavalry proprietors of their own arms—Remarks on the Affghans as irregular cavalry, and necessity of maintaining clan distinctions.

After my departure from the Saharunpore district the roving nature of my commission enabled me to observe the features of the revolt over an extensive tract of country; thus a slightly clearer idea of the drift and course of the mutiny in the native army, and its connection with actual rebellion, was gradually gleaned. Though mutiny and rebellion were unmistakeably united, still to those reasoning from a European point of view, the most irreconcilable contradictions constantly present themselves; and, indeed, it could not be otherwise where such contradictions and impulses as invariably appear in the native character, have an existence. That it was a rebellion as far as Hindustanis are capable of such an enterprise is clear to any one, taking into consideration the ordinary Hindustani idiosyncrasies; and that it was not one in the strictly European sense, was due to the very peculiarities of the Hindustani, which alone have enabled us to conquer and hold India. Nevertheless, had the native army not mutinied, rebellion would have been an impossibility.

Against the supposition of a rebellion, those who found their opinion on the facts placed before the English public, naturally advance instances of loyalty on the part of a few far-seeing native princes, landholders, and others, who understood the character of their own race sufficiently to foresee ultimate results; but, in fact, the loyalty of these men, with the difficulties and dangers attending it, only stands out in bold relief, rendering more prominent the universal rebellion round them. Amongst those, on the other hand, actually acquainted with the rebellious portions of the country, who believe only in mutiny, not in rebellion, is generally alleged the fact of the universal loyalty of the mass of the respectable population in the larger provincial towns; and that the intestine war amongst the villagers proved anarchy and rebellion, while instances exist of the more powerful even attacking Hindustanis and English indiscriminately.*

In the cities all but the low Mahomedan rabble were invariably in favour of order, but not of the English, if order could exist without them. The inhabitants of the larger cities being generally effeminate, and having considerable property at stake, were naturally averse to disorder, an interested loyalty hardly worthy the name. Again throughout the country certain classes of villages

* Thus a certain powerful Thakoor of Mahadewa called Gungoo Singh, having attacked some English refugees proceeding from Futtehgurh to Cawnpore in July, 1857, was seized for this offence and sentenced by me to twenty-one years' transportation. Amongst other escapades, shortly after this attack on the English party, he had laid siege to the city of Kunouj, from which he was obliged to beat a retreat, after his force had suffered considerable loss. This did not, however, satisfy him. At a still later date he amused himself by defying the chief rebel power in his neighbourhood, as will be seen from the following paper. The document is an order from the Nawab of Furruckabad addressed to Mahomed Moosun Alli Khân, his nazim or lieutenant-governor of the eastern district and commander of the forces there, to punish Master Gungoo Singh. The order runs thus :—" A petition from Our Thanahdar of Mahomdabad has been received, informing Us that he had been obliged to remove a police force (stationed on the right bank of the Ganges), in consequence of a gun belonging to Gungoo Singh, Thakoor of Mahadewa, playing on them (from the left bank of the river), You (the Nazim) are ordered to punish Gungoo L. Singh. Dated September 23, 1857."

attacked and destroyed certain other classes; but this is an ingrained characteristic of the Hindustani, a fact amply illustrated throughout the history of India. States are but reflections of the character of the mass of the population within their limits, and Indian kingdoms have invariably been short-sighted and selfish in their policy; the objectless animosities of these States being taken advantage of by the East India Company to conquer the country. On a smaller scale the very same animosities exist among neighbouring villages, and can be equally taken advantage of when necessary. Hindustani instincts overruling all other considerations, the moment British power was paralysed, free scope being given to the indulgence of these petty animosities, no ulterior objects restrained the villagers. Rebellion, though universal, thus became far from national in the European sense, unless the universal hatred of the English may be said to give it a national colouring. The villagers generally looked little beyond their own immediate circle, and this is one of the most important weaknesses in the native character, which with reasonable care will always enable us to keep in check the peasantry and the smaller class of zemindars who compose the great mass of the population. Yet in the midst of these intestine wars had a white face unbacked by power appeared, all these discordant elements would, in almost every instance, have united for his destruction, and then again set about their own. I myself, as the foregoing pages may illustrate, took advantage successfully of race animosities; but my movements were on these occasions invariably much trammelled, in consequence of a feeling of suspicion that the still stronger race antipathies of conquered *versus* conqueror, might manifest themselves, being well aware of the universal feeling existing against us. The Hindustanis in fact now hate us, and will continue to do so to the end of the chapter, however pleased and contented they appear to be with our rule and its unmistakeable benefits, for never did any subject race but detest its conquerors. The Hindustani is simply wanting in steady energy, and not demonstrative, but a deep rooted sluggish hatred exists, and it will always evince itself when opportunity offers. We can never again flatter ourselves that we are liked, or ever can be so, though at first we were doubtless looked upon in the light of deliverers, not of conquerors. Although kind and indulgent to the Hindustani, we must now always continue on our guard, however calm the surface.

There is one remarkable feature in this rebellion that has hardly been noticed, at any rate as it should have been, as on it depend consequences which may hereafter be fatal to our existence in Northern India. In the formation of our native army which is to assist in holding India, and without which it is clear that we should be unable to do so, a vital error was formerly committed in not recruiting according to nationalities, and this mistake is now being repeated in that recent manufacture called the military police.

Even within the circle of the North-West Provinces there exist several marked nationalities; and though in 1857 the whole country when in open revolt was apparently acting with one national will under separate leaders, this was far from the case in reality. These leaders had none of them any united or matured plan of co-operation, for a united nationality was beyond their comprehension, and many of them, though previous to the outbreak always intriguing, had intrigued so long unsuccessfully, that they knew little more of coming events than rumour informed them; certainly they never suspected that the revolt would approach so near to success as it eventually did. The majority, in fact, of these rebel chiefs became the representatives of nationalities almost without their own knowledge, being elected leaders by the few active spirits who originated and organized the movement in various localities, procuring the universal assent of all the influential zemindars, without whose passive, and at times active co-operation, they could not have held their own. These nationalities which thus sprung into existence never had the remotest intention or wish to re-unite, either under the kings of Delhi or Lucknow, though they exchanged civilities with both, even to the acknowledgment of their supremacy;

but had our power actually ceased to exist, they would soon have been engaged in hostilities with each other. How thoroughly without any national sentiment of union against the common foe were even the most prominent leaders of the rebels up to the moment when disaster was staring them in the face, will appear from the following.

On the fall of Delhi, Mahomed Bukt Khân, the commander-in-chief of the rebel forces in that city, had fled to Furruckabad with all the few men he could keep together. Here they were by no means well received, but were called upon to pay their way, and seem to have found considerable difficulty in obtaining the ordinary means of subsistence. On the advance of the British forces Mahomed Bukt Khân joined Moosun Alli Khân, one of the nazims of the Nawab of Furruckabad, in opposing the British, and on being defeated at Khoodagunge, he was making the best of his way across the Ganges. At this moment of all others, when the Nawab of Furruckabad must have seen with the most unpleasant clearness the prospect of an instantaneous reoccupation of the seat of his government by the British, from which he himself fled in a few days, he issued on the 25th of December, 1857, the following order to Likha Singh, talookdar of Allahgunge:—

"Mahomed Bukt Khân with his companions in arms, being in the possession of five or six lacs of rupees, is fleeing before the Europeans, therefore, to

Us the all-powerful, this appears right that you plunder all the cash and personal effects of Bukt Khân and his companions. You will not be called to account for this pillaging, but the guns, magazine, and elephants attached to his force you are to send in to Us, that We being pleased, it may be to your advantage. This is written as an injunction. You are to act strictly as you are ordered." *

This order recalls to mind the tactics of certain of the inferior breed of dogs which invariably turn on

* This paper, along with others of greater or less importance, was sent to me by the talookdar of Allahgunge, the man here mentioned. The messenger who brought it delivered it to me as an earnest of his master's wish to come to terms with our Government; but as my acceptance of the documents seemed likely to compromise the Government in any future proceedings against the man when seized, the papers were returned to him after I had taken a translation of this document merely as a curiosity. The infatuation with which the rebels preserved all their records is remarkable enough; and in many instances, though their destruction could have been simply accomplished, on no account would they permit this sacrilege. This objection to destroy a paper bearing any inscription originates in certain Mahomedan sentiments, with which all Christians can sympathise, and which the Hindoos have imbibed along with many other more objectionable Mahomedan prejudices, while the Mahomedans have adopted some that essentially belonged to Hindooism. The Mahomedan will never at random destroy any written document from the possibility that the name of God may happen to have been inscribed thereon; the Hindoos have followed suit, and object to the destruction of documents, lest they should contain the name of their particular protecting deity. These prejudices assisting, it is extraordinary what an amount of documentary evidence existed against most of the leading rebels. If any one understanding the subject would take the trouble, and had time to run through these papers, a most interesting account of the revolt might be compiled.

any of their cherished companions when receiving a castigation.

The facility with which the native races split up into nationalities under leaders selfishly interested was one great cause of their incomprehensible bungling in not uniting for our expulsion, illustrating again, on a larger scale, the same inherent disregard for national interests evinced by the village communities. In the country north and north-west of Allahabad, the Nana was probably the only instance in which the various races, in almost every district, did not acknowledge the descendants of their former rulers; and, as far as the confusion would admit, the ancient boundaries of the tracts were at once claimed and acknowledged with the most regal etiquette. From correspondence, however, that passed through my hands, I noticed that, as early as July, 1857, the germs of discord were springing up on this very subject of territorial jurisdiction.* From this, their own classification of races, we might derive a valuable lesson, enabling us to define the recruiting boun

* The following is a portion of a correspondence addressed by the Nana from the south to Ghose Alli, the tuhseeldar of Tirrua Tutheea, and by the Nawab of Furruckabad from the north, to the same intelligent, native official of the British Government, whose answers to the opposing claimants of the Tuhseelee under his charge are strikingly honest and sensible. Ghose Alli, as a servant of the British Government, placed between two hostile rebel leaders, found himself in by no means a pleasant position, and one that would have puzzled most men, as disloyalty to any of his three masters might have resulted in his ruin. The first

daries of each regiment in the native army. Had our old sepoy army been thus recruited from certain depôts alone, and the men of each regiment raised

paper is an order from the Nana, addressed to Ghose Alli, tuhseeldar of Tirrua Tutheea, dated Bithoor, June 29th, 1857:—

LETTER NO. 1.

"As by the bounty of God, this kingdom with its wealth, the gift of the Almighty, has fallen into my hands, therefore you are ordered to forward to our government all the money in the Tirrua Tutheea Tuhseelee. You are to continue to discharge your duties as formerly, and see that there is no discontinuance of the same, and that the subjects are not injured by plunderers. We also will appear to perfect all arrangements; and if any subjects are being injured, we will give them justice. You are to proclaim in your neighbourhood the assumption of power by this Government, and whoever desires justice, he is to present himself at our Durbar; and if this is not done, his complaints will not hereafter be heard, as, besides dismissal of his suit, such a one will not obtain justice. Looking with dread on us, at once forward the government money, with the accounts of the same, immediately on the receipt of this order; and if you disobey, you may bring your trembling hand to your teeth; you had better at once become the humble servant of this our Government; if you have any other intentions, you had better erase them from your mind. Understand this as an urgent order."

To the above, Ghose Alli, the tuhseeldar, sends the following answer to the Nana, dated July 5th, 1857:—

LETTER NO. 2.

"We were all delighted on receiving your orders; may the Lord daily prosper you! The state of affairs as regards the money in the Tuhseelee is this, that 10,749 Company's rupees remained in the Tuhseelee on the 15th May. When these disturbances commenced, on my own responsibility, in case of further disturbances, I handed over the money in the Tuhseelee to Rajah Phokur Singh, of Tutheea; after which I received Mr. Probyn's order to hand it over to the Ranee, 'Princess' of Tirrua. Mr. Probyn also wrote to the Ranee on the subject. In accordance with that order, I took the money back from Rajah Phokur Singh, delivering it from localities defined by the natural territorial limits and sympathies of the various races, the universal mutiny that has occurred would in all pro-

over to the Ranee. I sent the receipt to the magistrate, and the Ranee also wrote a letter regarding the receipt of the money. The magistrate also ordered me to entertain thirty additional police, for whose expenses 100 rupees were retained in the Tuhseelee, and intimation sent to the magistrate, consequently only 3 rupees remain in the Tuhseelee. When the disturbances commenced, all the police fled, and only nineteen recently entertained orderlies and office writers are present with me, nor are these properly armed. I possess no authority in the disposal of the treasure in the possession of the Ranee; but she has no objections to surrender the money to the Government of the day, therefore your honour had better issue your orders to the Ranee. First, the Ranee will not give up the money to me without your orders; and next, I have no guard under whose protection it could be forwarded to your Highness. In consequence of the receipt of your order, the proclamation has been issued; but in this neighbourhood for 20 coss (40 miles) in length, by 9 coss in breadth, the disturbances will not cease without the appearance of guns and an army. In consequence of the disturbed state of the country and absence of regular posts, I cannot forward the daily reports every day, but I have no wish to disobey your orders; I am an old servant and an honourable man. I again repeat, however, that regarding the treasure, you must issue an order to the Ranee, and send troops to escort it."

The Nana again addressed Ghose Alli on the 8th of July, 1857:—

LETTER No. 3.

"Your petition of the 5th of July, expressing a hope that orders would be issued to the Ranee regarding the disposal of the treasure, has been perused. In accordance with your request, an order has been issued to the Ranee, and officers with detachments of infantry and cavalry are being despatched to bring the treasure. For the better arrangement of your country, you are to entertain ten additional horsemen, with a hundred badge-bearers, old and new servants—but take care that both old and new servants together be not more numerous; and money to pay the office-clerks, bability not only never have taken place, but the races might have been successfully brought to act against each other. Thus, early in the mutiny,

you are to take from the revenue collections after the troops arrive."

To the above letter No. 3, Ghose Alli sends the following answer to the Nana, dated July 13th, 1857:—

LETTER NO. 4.

"In my former petition I told you my position, but I would prefer that you would accept my resignation. Your best plan would be to write to the Nawab of Furruckabad, as it appears from an order of the Nawab's that a force has been despatched by him to remove the treasure, and a notice to this effect has also been issued to the Ranee. I forward to you a copy of this order, as also of one to the Ranee."

The following is one of the letters addressed by the Nawab of Furruckabad to Ghose Alli, which, doubtless, elicited the letter No. 4 to the Nana:—

LETTER NO. 5.

"As 10,600 rupees of the May and June collections are in the hands of the Ranee, detachments of infantry and cavalry will be sent to remove this treasure, and you are to procure its delivery from the Ranee, as through your agency it was originally collected. Take care that there is no delay, or it will not be to your advantage. You and the office-clerks are to consider yourselves our servants; you are to collect the revenue, make good arrangements, send lists of the government servants, and if you require assistance, send word. Dated July 12th, 1857."

The following is Ghose Alli's reply to this order from the Nawab of Furrackabad, and is dated on the same day as the letter No. 4 to the Nana:—

LETTER NO. 6.

"On the receipt of your order regarding the treasure, I immediately sent the order in charge of a horseman to the Ranee. Before the arrival of this order, a similar order was issued by the Nana Sahib, Peshwah Bahador, who was informed by me that the money had been delivered over to the Ranee; an order also came in the Ranee's name. I possess no power in the disposal of the many of the Rhajpore sepoys held aloof, and received no kind of sympathy from the Oude sepoys, though they afterwards joined them heart and soul, in consequence of being so completely mixed up with them, and in a minority. For instance, the majority of the 10th Native Infantry, who were Bhojpooreeas, left Futtehgurh for their own country, when the 41st Native Infantry, who had been recruited chiefly in Oude, arrived at Futtehgurh;* and in their march

money; however, the Ranee has no objections to surrender it; but as two Governments have demanded this money, the Ranee wishes that the difficulty should be decided by a correspondence with the Nana, particularly as this country belongs to Furruckabad, and the money should be sent there. After an amicable arrangement, the Ranee will act as decided. I now forward a copy of the Nana's order, but I am powerless in the matter of the treasure. My police have fled, anarchy surrounds us, and we sit with shut doors. You must settle difficulties with the Nana. To restore quiet in the district, a company or two of sepoys, with cavalry and a gun, should be sent us; without this, peace will be an impossibility. Dated July 13th, 1857."

The above correspondence shows that if the native potentates had been left to their own devices, the forces of the Nana and Nawab would soon have come into collision regarding the disputed jurisdiction of Tirrua Tutheea; but a third party stepping in, the Nana is kicked out of Bithoor, and the Nawab quietly secures the treasure with the disputed tract of country, while our friend, Ghose Alli, retires into private life.

* The following is a translation made by a clerk in the Delhi commissioner's office of a document found in the palace after the fall of Delhi, and forwarded to me by the commissioner when I was preparing the case for the prosecution against the Nawab of Furruckabad. This paper is important, as determining how far the 10th Native Infantry were actually divided into two parties—the mutineers belonging to Oude or Furruckabad, the loyal being Bhojpooreeas. This native account may also help to prove if a judicious division of those races had been preserved, they might

through Oude, near the left bank of the Ganges, the 10th Native Infantry were so harassed and cut up by the Oude population, as to be obliged to retreat

have been induced to act against each other. Had the 10th, in fact, consisted only of Bhojpooreeas, they would have been strong enough to resist the 41st (Dobâee) Native Infantry, which a small party of them actually did on their account, and were killed or driven out of the place by the 41st.

"In the name of God, the Benevolent and Merciful.

"The throne of the God-bestowed Government made prosperous. May the shadow of God remain on your God-sent Majesty! may you always enjoy sovereignty and wealth! Sacrificers of our lives, of servant-like behaviour, carpet-bearers in manner, like disciples, We, Sheo Gholam Ditchet, Soobahdars, and other officers and sepoys of Dobâee (*i.e.*, 41st Regiment Native Infantry), after going through the usual forms of respect on the threshold high as heaven to the courtiers of great and excellent honour, are employed in the representing of circumstances worthy of relation, and they are these:—

"That on Monday, the 8th Showal, 1,273 Hidjree, when the sun of good fortune of the malignant Kafirs at the station of Seetapore was darkened in the first place at the hour of ten A.M., the chief officer or colonel of the regiment, who was also brigadier of the above-mentioned station, together with five Englishmen, entered hell by the musketry of the sepoys. After this, the Nazarenes of bad religion (*i.e.*, the collector and commissioner), and others who had fled from other districts, and were unfortunately living in the above station, all to the number of nearly forty bad men, by the muskets of brave men of heroic conduct became travellers to hell. After that, in the middle of the road, at Arungabad, in the district of Mohumdee, which is at the distance of twenty-two coss from Seetapore, thirty-four men of vile character, by musketry and sword-cuts were made travellers to hell. After that, making choice of the fatigue of the march, we became desirous of kissing the threshold of your Majesty. On reaching Shahjehanpore, we heard from reliable men that the Dufful (10th Regiment Native Infantry) was separated into two parties, that half are enemies to religion, in other words, leaving the straight road are in every way well-wishers of the Kafirs, and the other half, being firm across the Ganges. The same kind of enmity divides the Delhi territory and Rohilkund, where, with the exception of the Mahomedans of both places, no kindred tie of any description exists.

For the advantage of those among my readers not acquainted with the localities, the nationalities

and resolved on their own religion, have Delhi for their object. Although the straight road to Delhi was through Bareilly, yet with the object of helping the other half of the 10th Native Infantry leaving Shahjehanpore, we arrived at Furruckabad.

"A wonderful circumstance happened when we arrived at Furruckabad. That on the first day all the sepoys and officers of the mutinous regiment, with joy meeting us separately, agreed to kill the Kafirs, and to take away the treasure and magazine to Delhi. It again happened that part of the above-mentioned regiment setting their forces against us, divided part of the treasure amongst themselves, and taking the remainder to the Nazarenes in the Futtehgurh Fort, prepared themselves to fight with us, and without delay made ready the artillery. The servants of the King, not thinking of the power of those bad conducted and fearless men, suddenly became the attacking party, killed a number with the sword, besides twenty of their muskets and a flag came into the possession of your Majesty. After that, the unclean Nazarenes, with the magazine, treasure, and other stores, with the help of the above-mentioned regiment, took refuge in the fort, and were all as proud as Pharaoh. Since the killing of them was necessary, moreover decreed by God, at that time the well-wishers of your Majesty, strengthening their promise and agreement, having surrounded the fort, attacked the heights and bastions from every side, and the unclean Kafirs, also bringing vain bravery into play, kept off the warriors with grape and musketry; but until when? According to the tradition, 'To make religious war on the Kafirs,' the tried warriors, not considering their vain bravery, and not counting the dead and wounded, a second and a third time attacked the fort. At last, from the surrounding of the fort, after fifteen days, by the contrivances of mines and ladders, we reduced the defenders to great straits. Then the malignant ones, in the middle of that night, being conquered and seized with fear, having defined by the revolt in the tract above Cawnpore might be classed under four great heads: 1. The districts known as the old Delhi territory; 2. Rohilkund; 3. The territory formerly possessed by the Bungush family, represented by the Nawab of Furruckabad; and, 4. The Oude kingdom, or rather

gone out of the fort, secretly getting on board boats, took the way of the river, and the Jahadees (fanatic followers of the flag of Mahomed), accounting their safe departure to be a shame on themselves, followed them by land and water; and, at a distance of five or six coss (twelve miles) from the fort, surrounded them in the river, and by means of guns and swords made them run to hell, and six persons, women and children, who came as prisoners, were made over to the chief of Furruckabad. Several of us, the Jahadees of the 41st Regiment Native Infantry, of the 10th Nizamut, and Irregular Cavalry, were killed or wounded.

"And before this petition we had previously sent a petition by the hands of a messenger to your Majesty; doubtless it has met with your noble perusal. The chief of Furruckabad in assistance, and providing supplies in every instance, used his utmost endeavours, and the excuse for the absence of the regiment is owing to the wounded. And in these days that Nana Rao was employed with forces and Jahadees in the establishment of Cawnpore, and Cawnpore had also been purified of the presence of the unclean, but in consequence of the junction of certain bad men and ignorant sepoys, who had committed the greatest perfidy against Nana Rao, again the Kafirs, to the number of nearly 500 unfortunate Europeans and 300 Seikhs, are living in Cawnpore; and from messengers we hear that the unclean intend destroying Furruckabad; for this reason we have remained longer. Whatever order, however, may be issued by your Majesty, will be acted upon. Another fact is this, that a man named Moulvie, colour rather fair, English eyes, wearing the coloured clothes of a mendicant, went into the camp of Cawnpore; and having joined with the sepoys, sowed dissensions, and now with 150 troopers has started for Delhi."

A term of blessing ends this petition of Sheo Gholam, with the soobahdars, and other officers of the regiments, Dobâee, Nizamut, and Hyderee Cavalry.

such portion of the old Oude Nawabee, not embracing Rohilkund or Furruckabad, as were conquests made by the Nawabee. These appear to have been the great race classifications of this part of the country; and, though several small rajahs and nawabs sprung into existence, they would soon, if left alone, have been extinguished by the more powerful. During my investigation of sepoy cases, nothing astonished me more than the total neglect of the first principles to be observed by a conquering race when raising an army from the conquered.

Each recruiting officer had his own peculiar fancies or whims regarding castes and races; so that regiments were fortunate if, in a few years, they did not become the most complete jumble of races that could possibly exist. It is only marvellous that this frail fabric, filled with combustible materials, with an important Seikh element in each regiment, did not create more extended mischief or mutiny earlier than it did. As if to cut our own throats the more effectually, and render the whole of India as much as possible one nationality, I found, in the trials held by me, that not only was the Seikh element incorporated into a Hindustani army, and *vice versâ*, but Hindustanis were swarming in the Bombay army, in the Scinde irregular force, in the regiments supposed to be Beloochees, in the Nizam's contingent (a Madras force), and throughout the Central Indian contingents; so that the Hindustanis of the North-West Provinces and Oude had actually become the soldiers for the major portion of our Indian empire—an unmistakeable proof of the active warlike propensities of this race. An enormous number, too, of these Hindustanis thus distributed were Puthans, the class of all others the most hostile to English rule, and who will never cease to be so. If enlisted at all, these Puthans of Rohilkund and the Ganges-Jumna Doab should be kept in distinct regiments, and not mixed up in, and allowed to intrigue as formerly with, the whole nativ army.

Disregard of nationalities previous to the last revolt, at one time, very nearly effected our ruin, and it is to be hoped we shall not again plunge into the same erroneous misconception of our own interests. In the formation of the local irregular forces raised after the annexation of the Punjaub and Oude, which were supposed to be recruited from those countries alone, though the infantry were generally of the race with which they possessed kindred, the cavalry certainly were not, which, as might be expected, led to much confusion the moment the revolt broke out. As an example of the inconvenience here alluded to, it was necessary to divide the 1st Punjaub Cavalry into two wings, one of which, as, being composed of Seikhs and Affghans, it could be trusted at Delhi, was sent there; but the head-quarters of the regiment, composed chiefly of Hindustanis, as being untrustworthy, were eventually sent to us at Saharunpore, where some of the men deserted near Thanah Bhawun; while the remainder were a cause of constant anxiety to their officers. It was this blending of Seikhs in Hindustani regiments, and *vice versâ*, that so very nearly seduced the Seikhs to fraternize with the Hindustanis, which would have become an accomplished fact had Delhi held out much longer. Again, the history of the Nusseeree Goorkhas, given pretty fully in this book, should show that, had Goorkhas and Hindustanis been mixed in our regiments, all the former, jealous in the extreme of their caste, would probably have turned against us—and a feather, though this would have been a heavy one, may break the camel's back.

Turning next to Oude, we see that the system—or rather the want of it—there adopted, in recruiting local irregular cavalry regiments produced serious consequences. Those even in authority seemed totally ignorant of the fact that this Oude irregular cavalry was chiefly composed of Puthans from the Mow Shumshabad and Rohilkund districts, or residents of the old Delhi territory; so that, when the mutiny broke out in the north, with a mixture of infatuation and ignorance, some of these regiments were moved up from Lucknow towards Allygurh and Agra, where, being placed conveniently in the midst of their mutinous brethren, the usual sad conclusion, mutiny, accompanied by the murder of their officers, rapidly resulted; while the only chance of keeping these irregulars loyal, had the component elements been known, would have been to retain them in the Oude territory, or send them south. The system of recruiting had, however, become so completely a matter of chance, that even those who should have been best acquainted with the subject were ignorant of the nationality of these local Oude regiments; and the mistake will again occur, if the local regiments are to be local in name only, and not in substance.

Independently of a strict attention to the nationalities, to me it seems important that even the two creeds of Mahomedan and Hindoo should not be mingled in native regiments; for in the old native army, by annihilating a distinction which formerly caused much jealousy and disunion, we united both classes against us in the late revolt. By making the distinction of Mahomedan and Hindoo regiments, the management of the individual regiments may become a little more difficult, but the army thus constituted will be less likely to unite against us. At any rate, the Hindoos might generally be found willing to oppose Mahomedans, though it will always be an object with the latter to prevent such a collision.

Even high-caste and low-caste Hindoos should not be united in one regiment. Here religion and ancient prejudices at once come into play, and the low caste continues the obedient slave of the high caste. Place high castes alone in one regiment, low castes alone in another, and combination will give the latter strength for freedom of action. Low-caste regiments, formed entirely of Bhunghies and Chumars, will, after a while, face, if necessary, any high-caste regiment, and would, very likely, thrash them, as the Bhunghies generally proved themselves more than a match for the Rajpoots in all their petty fights throughout the revolt. Still, by all means, enlist high-caste regiments, for it is as well that the Government should not seem to the natives to associate itself entirely with what the conquered race consider the dregs of the population; though it will eventually be a matter of less difficulty to raise these low castes in the scale of civilization than the prejudiced high castes, who are, doubtless, at present far in advance of the classes over whom they exercise such an extraordinary influence.

This commingling of castes has already borne fruit in our new native army. Of the new levies raised since our reoccupation of the Ganges-Jumna Doab, one regiment was sent out with the column reoccupying the south-west of Oude, or rather that portion of it situated in the vicinity of Sundee. After we had quietly resumed possession of the country, on Christmas day, 1858, the European soldiers improvised some athletic games, in which their newly raised native companions in arms, with the residents of the surrounding country, were invited to join. Amongst other things, a small prize surmounted a greased pole, which natives, as well as Europeans, were ambitious to reach. This was, however, as all the natives knew, Christmas day, the great festival of the Christians. A greased pole had actually been erected, being only a step in advance of the greased cartridge, and though the natives had of their own accord assembled, assuming an air of enjoyment to show their loyalty, they were gaping wide with suspicion. A native happened to be attempting the feat of ascending the pole, when it accidentally broke, and fell with him to the ground. Instantly every Hindustani took to flight, and before the Europeans could divine what was up, hardly one was to be seen in the neighbourhood. The Europeans had joined in the games with the new levy and other natives without even their side-arms; yet the latter, to judge from their precipitate flight, must have supposed that this accident was a signal for a general massacre.

Whatever the real cause of this panic, the incident shows that the new army may not turn out superior to, or a whit less suspicious than, the old one, if the same imprudence in the disposal of the castes continues. In fact, the old entirely high-caste regiments were infinitely superior to the present experiment of mixing high and low castes. As has been before observed, caste prejudice in the North-West Provinces means the very religion of the country; and not only that, but it constitutes the holy of holies in that religion. Until Christianity or some other belief supersedes the present religion, it is simply impossible to ignore caste with its absurd, yet dangerous, results. In the new levy referred to, there were Bhunghies and other low castes, who would, if alone, have rather delighted than objected to a greased pole. But in the same regiment must needs be placed an allotment of Gwallas and other castes, notorious for their caste prejudices, and whose noble example, when associated with low castes, the latter would naturally and blindly follow.

Though objections may be raised to the present disposal of castes, Lord Clyde, when creating the new levies, had the sound sense to insist on their being locals with permanent recruiting depôts. It is to be hoped that this arrangement may not be upset. But even supposing that this fortunate advance in the right direction be approved of, great and unceasing vigilance will still be required in seeing that the men recruited at each depôt are actually residents of the locality to which they profess to belong, and that their caste and relations' names have not been falsely entered. Nothing gave me more difficulty in investigating the cases of mutineers than this universal system of false entries adopted by the sepoys of the old army, whom it was often more difficult to identify when the records were forthcoming than when they had been destroyed; and there could not have been any other object in thus enlisting under false colours than that of evading justice in the event of misconduct. The feeling of security arising from the knowledge of being falsely registered had doubtless much to do with the wild recklessness with which many knowing hands entered into mutiny, subsequently taking uncommonly good care not to expose their precious persons to any danger.

By decreeing severe penalties, and introducing new checks connected with the recruiting office, it will be very easy to prevent this wholesale falsification; and the Hindustani will probably look before he leaps next time, when the certainty of ultimate detection will stare him in the face. That these checks are necessary is obvious, this system of falsification having already recommenced. When I was investigating the cases of some sepoys belonging to the new Bunares military police, the falsification either in caste, locality, or names of relations, was almost universal; and some I was eventually obliged to release under the terms of the amnesty, totally unable to discover their real abodes. This falsification also existed in another military police force, where, on mentioning the subject to the officer commanding, he soon discovered a considerable party of Brahmuns, who had enlisted as belonging to inferior castes. Though these two cases happen to refer to the new military police alone, I have not the least doubt that this falsification will be found to exist largely in the new army levies which were very hurriedly collected much after former precedents. But to make Jack Sepoy feel how thoroughly he is in our power, which must now become the very essence of our influence over him, not only should this falsification be provided against, but a copy of all regimental records should be filed at head-quarters, or in any forts under the charge of Europeans, so that we may not again witness the evaporation of almost all traces of the mutineers on the mutiny of a regiment.

The system of permitting the irregular cavalry to become the proprietors of their own arms, generally the best that England can produce, with which they return to their homes, is an antiquated error, and should be abolished, or we may constantly see European officers, led by a very laudable *esprit de corps*, as in one of the Southern Marhattah Horse, desiring to furnish their men with the wondrous armament of swords, double-barrelled carbines, and revolvers, which the natives are always willing enough to purchase if to become their absolute property. In this branch of the service, one of the most important towards the efficiency of a European force when taking the field in a tropical climate, no finer body of irregular cavalry could be raised than the Affghans, who would willingly take service in larger numbers than at present permitted, and might be depended upon to continue loyal as long as we abstained from conquering their country, and secured them small retiring pensions. Guaranteeing their independence while enlisting their services, we should not only secure a force which might be depended upon for repressive purposes in India, but in the event of invasion from the north-west frontier, the only point from which an invasion could possibly come, as long as we are masters of the sea, the Affghans would form an interested barrier of trained men, both themselves and families keenly alive to the danger of losing their independence and their pensions. But even when enlisting these wild tribes, caution is necessary in keeping the various clans distinct, that the traditionary animosities and distrusts existing amongst them be not softened. Here again, however, disarm every Affghan returning to his own country, or we may find the weapons with which we furnish them employed against ourselves.

In a word, whatever materials are selected, the very heart and soul of our policy in forming a native army in India should, under any circumstances, be *divide et impera*, not only in the case of nationalities, but also with creeds and castes. Nor does it seem possible to conceive how, with the experience of 1857 before us, any other conclusion could be arrived at, particularly with reference to a strict definition of nationalities as carried out by the adoption of local regiments in the army, while a contrary policy would, if adopted, seem to be dictated alone by that infatuation so often depicted as taking possession of the doomed.*

* The following capitation is from the Report of the Commissioners appointed to inquire into the Organization of the Indian Army, clause i. p. xiv.—"That the native army should be composed of different nationalities and castes, and as a general rule, *mixed promiscuously* through each regiment."

CHAPTER XII.

Outline of the origin of the revolt in the North-Western Provinces of India in 1857.

DURING the progress of the Indian revolt in 1857, accident placed me in possession of General Pepe's account of the Italian revolutions in 1848-49, and being much struck by his picture of the origin of that revolt, which appeared singularly applicable to the development of the rebellion in the North-West Provinces, I give the following extract, though, as in the Indian, there was probably more of design in the Italian revolt than General Pepe has thought it politic to divulge.

General Pepe, who commanded one of the Italian contingents, remarks that:—"Revolutions being prepared by a certain invisible process in the secret depths of men's minds, their execution depends on an instantaneous concord of divers causes, and a spontaneous combination of will and power, the production of which is ever determined by unforeseen circumstances, and escapes all forecast respecting the precise moment in which it will be effected."

The "divers causes" existing in and exciting the

various localities in the North-West Provinces, whose "instantaneous concord" and "spontaneous combination" produced the explosion there in 1857, were certainly numerous enough, many of them apparently of trifling import, not extending beyond a very contracted sphere, and peculiarly local in their complexion; so much so, in fact, that, if in any case they were unassociated with the general features of the revolt, these specialities led to exactly opposite conclusions. But let the conclusions be what they may in isolated cases, the motive force of the whole, exciting the direct causes which developed the plot, and which, in the confusion of the outbreak, obscured the real causes, may be described as a feeling of universal opposition to the English rule and religion. The following is a rough outline of what appeared to me, from such information as I could collect, to be the principal agencies employed in producing this universal feeling of more than distrust, resulting in a "spontaneous combination" against us.

On minutely examining the early history of our conquests in India, it will be seen that the men who gave England her first firm grasp in the Peninsula found it necessary to act without the aid of European troops, which England was not then in a position to supply; and if conquest could not have been effected without their assistance, our present position in India would probably not have been very dissimilar from that which has been achieved in China. To effect their purpose of extending and securing our possessions, those clear-sighted men exerted every influence to propitiate the Brahmuns, through whose agency each successive step, either in peace, in war, or in negotiation, was transacted. But a race of rulers succeeded incapable of appreciating the soundness of this policy, by whom the Mahomedans were propitiated and the Brahmuns ignored. The new régime seemed ignorant that the latter, though dictating the tone of public opinion amongst the Hindoos, are, while not directly interfered with, singularly tolerant to all other creeds, and, if in power, will induce their co-religionists to submit to innovations which it would otherwise be extremely dangerous to introduce; the Brahmun himself being infinitely less influenced by caste prejudices than nine-tenths of the Hindoo population. On the other hand, those who changed our policy appear to have been equally unconscious of the fact, that nothing can temper the aggressive hate of Mahomedanism, though, with a fascinating and gentlemanly semblance of friendship, it may bide its time till it fancies the spring may be taken with certainty. Not till the opening of the revolt did this Anglo-Mahomedan régime discover that they had been nursing the most implacable of enemies, whose unvarying watchword had ever been embodied in the maxim—"To extinguish a fire, leave not a spark; to extirpate snakes, spare not their young;" a significant precept which will continue to represent the inherent instinct of Mahomedanism while it exists and possesses the power of action.

The Brahmuns ignored, and the Mahomedans not propitiated, a false move had doubtless been made, engendering discontent; and, though not of a serious character, it was a policy which possessed no counter-balancing advantage. The Brahmuns, after a short time, did not probably trouble their heads much about it, but set to work increasing their influence in other directions. In this endeavour they had succeeded so far as to make themselves a comfortable position, when we again stepped in to interfere with what this class now considered their vested rights and interests in the people. English civilization and Hindoo prejudices thus brought into conflict, it was self-evident that one or the other must give in, and this the Brahmuns of Bengal were not prepared to do.

The Brahmuns of the North-West Provinces, as far as I could ever discover, though cunning calculators, are by no means that dangerous class of *intriguants* which the Cóleens and other subdivisions of this race appear to be in Bengal Proper. The Cóleens, though they originally migrated from Kunouj in the North-West Provinces, have, from finding themselves thrown amongst a much inferior race, assumed a more prominent position than their brethren in the North-West, while, in consequence of their vicinity to the fountain-head of legislation, they have always restlessly watched its progress.

Had this astute body of men not initiated them into the facts, the Brahmuns, Chutrees, and Rajpoots of the North-West might never have observed or troubled their heads regarding any extent of legislation carried on in Calcutta, so long, at least, as the English Government did not interfere with their land tenures, as serious a question—or more serious, perhaps—than caste itself. But the Brahmuns of Calcutta, being well up in the legislation of the day which affected the free development of many of their disgraceful privileges, determined, if not to revenge themselves, at least to excite such a national feeling that the Government would be induced to pause in its course. To effect this, their Brahmun brethren in the North-West were set in motion to rouse the caste jealousies of their countrymen, more particularly of the sepoys; and all the more intelligent Brahmuns of the North-West whom I had an opportunity of questioning on the subject, declared that their own caste in the North-West had been led astray by the Bengal Brahmuns. This may or may not have been the case; but as agents or principals, in the excitement of caste prejudice at least, the Brahmuns of the North-West actively assisted in laying the train, and this taking effect, brings us to that stage of popular feeling when the whole country had become suspicious that some undefined action on the part of the Government was undermining their religion.

Coexistent with—in fact, almost antecedent to—this

caste agitation had gradually been springing up another agency, entirely of our own creation, which was silently undermining our influence over the subject population, and which very materially assisted the development of the caste movement. With the advance of our power in the Indian peninsula, we began to exercise a considerable control over the native States. The native being absolutely secure and independent in our own dominions, and the native princes, in the treatment of their subjects, being overawed into reason by the East India Company, the oppression also formerly existing in these native States surrounding them having thus ceased to act as a salutary warning to our own subjects, a generation gradually sprang up in our provinces, ignorant of the terrors of unrestrained native rule. Consequently, the mass of the population began to view the English in the light of conquerors, not of deliverers, as was very much the case when our incomprehensible success first dawned upon an ignorant and oppressed race. Tradition now glossed over the defects, and with its fascinating tales inspired a new charm to native rule, quickening the susceptibilities of a highly imaginative race. By a very natural transition, their minds were soon prepared to view their conquerors as conquerors alone, which decided, though undefined change, the influence and intrigue of the Brahmuns gradually extended, by producing that diseased state of deep jealousy and suspicion regarding their religion and caste, unhappily far exceeding the most sanguine expectations of the intriguers. With the mass of the population and army in this excitable condition, a step was determined upon by the British Government affecting not only Hindoos but Mahomedans; and so, by combining the two antagonistic creeds in one and the same cause against their conquerors, the crowning climax had arrived, and the explosion of popular feeling became merely a matter of opportunity.

Though the explosion could not, under any circumstances, have been long warded off, there can be but little doubt that the annexation of Oude exercised the greatest direct share in the mutiny and revolt of 1857, and this was invariably advanced to me in conversation by natives near the centres of revolt as the all-important cause, after other influences had paved the way throughout the territory belonging to the old Oude Nawabee* "viceroyalty" previous to 1801. But in the Delhi territory another chapter of intrigue was opened, of an almost purely Mahomedan type, though the caste and Oude grievances had here also their share as the necessary means of exciting the Nawabee sepoy, who was the agent

* The *Nawabee*, or viceroyalty of Oude, as it existed under the Mahomedan emperors previous to 1801, independently of that tract which the East India Company formed into the kingdom now known as Oude, comprised the districts of Goruckpore, Azimgurh, Allahabad, Futtehpore, Cawnpore, Etawa, Mynpoorie, Furruckabad, and the whole of Rohilkund, or, in other words, about half of the North-West Provinces.

in these scenes. Beyond the confines of these two tracts, other influences formed the incentive to revolt, which were, as previously stated, often extremely local in their complexion, and have given rise to much confusion in logically accounting for the revolt even amongst the higher class of natives themselves. Thus, nearer the Punjaub, frequently have I heard them attribute the mutiny to the fact, that the sepoys had gone "must," similar to a well-kept male elephant, in consequence of being too well cared for and not sufficiently worked; and this, like a great many other things, had its share. But Oude was the real stumbling-block of the day. Two-thirds of our sepoys being recruited either in Oude, or from those surrounding districts which tradition told them rightfully belonged to the old Nawabee, embracing, previous to the annexation of Oude, many of the richest districts in our possession, were all, though living under separate governments, connected by the closest ties of kindred and intermarriage, rendering them in every respect the same race, influenced by like prejudices or fears. Not unnaturally, then, all looked on the dethronement of the King of Oude in the same light as the Highlanders regarded the expulsion of the Stuarts, and by that step the feudal pride of a powerful, and, in some respects, an aristocratic army was deeply injured.

The usual statement, that their interests, being affected by the annexation, formed one very strong inducement to mutiny, would hardly seem to be well founded, for never did a class of men so recklessly cast their future prospects to the winds as these sepoys, even when placed in positions where escape after mutiny was almost hopeless. The King of Oude was regarded as the feudal chief, not only by the sepoys of modern Oude, but by those recruited in the ceded districts formerly belonging to the Nawabee "viceroyalty," and the infatuation in supporting a feudal chief is stronger at this day in India, particularly amongst Rajpoots and Chutrees, than it was amongst the Highlanders of Scotland in 1745.

I was some days with the force which advanced on Lucknow from Cawnpore in 1856, at the annexation of Oude. The secrecy and suddenness with which this large force appeared at Cawnpore, and, after being brigaded together a few days, marched on Lucknow, was certainly for the time a master-stroke, but its effect on the native mind was unmistakeable; even wealthy, fawning mahajuns could not conceal their sentiments regarding the act. If no other motive, however, influenced our movements, as a mere matter of self-defence the annexation of Oude had become absolutely necessary. The rising spirit of fanaticism which had lately manifested itself at Fyzabad and other places in Oude, might have spread through our own dominions, and must needs be checked. Nothing short of absorption could effect this. The fatal step, as all know, was not at the same time increasing our European force. But the natives, one and all, viewed this annexation as an act of the deepest treachery, and though at the time the native force employed loyally performed the duty it was called upon to discharge, from that day the whole Hindustani army was alienated. That the revolt did not then take place was owing entirely to the suddenness with which the measure was executed. Sudden as it was, however, and unprepared as the sepoys were to revolt, subsequent inquiries have convinced me, that had the King of Oude raised a finger the whole sepoy army would have risen to a man against their masters, and had the revolt then taken place, our position would have been even worse than it was in 1857.

But, independently of exciting the feudal pride of our native soldiery by the annexation of Oude, we also roused to its full activity the ever vindictive hate of a second class, as powerful in its organization as the sepoy army. The kingdom of Oude was viewed as the head of Mahomedanism in India by the largest portion of the followers of the Prophet in that country. They looked up to Lucknow as the most hopeful point from which the true believers should yet sally forth to turn the infidel Kafirs out of India, and establish the long-foretold Mahomedan supremacy. The annexation of Oude, by blasting those dearly cherished hopes, set in full motion these active intriguing spirits at a time when the persevering industry of the Bengal Brahmuns had produced distrust among the Hindoo population. From the date of this event the Brahminical influence begins to fade, or rather, to be lost sight of when obscured by the absorbing active intrigue of the Mahomedans, who, at once adopting the scheme initiated by the Brahmuns, carried it out with hearty good-will, and into better hands it could not have fallen. The Mahomedans knew that their co-religionists amongst the sepoys could be depended upon at all times. They saw that the feudal pride of the Hindoos had been deeply wounded, and it was determined to work this out through the still weaker point—the loss of caste, already the subject of anxious conversation throughout the army and country. But the army and people were already fully prepared to follow any leader. A well-matured plan of action was the only deficiency to be supplied: and the attempt to devise and carry out such a plan was made by the Mahomedans, the only men in the country capable of doing so, for their very religion rendered them an organized body not subject to the contradictions and uncertainties produced by caste distinctions amongst the Hindoos. There were certain Mahomedan rallying points throughout the North-West Provinces where secrecy and steadfast devotion to the common cause could be relied upon, with a connecting link of freemasonry, so to call it, uniting the smaller intervening Mahomedan communities.

The concentrative working power of such a body was enormous, and the whole Bengal army, already ripe for revolt, succumbed to their influence. As it turned out, they hardly embraced a large enough sphere, and their short-sighted contempt of the Seikhs, whom their vanity led them to suppose they had conquered in the Punjaub campaigns, proved their ruin. Had the alliance of the Seikhs prior to the outbreak been judiciously courted by the Hindustani Mahomedans, hardly a European would have escaped in all Northern India. But though the concentrative power of intrigue and organization was so great, far otherwise was that of action when the plot was developed. Immediately on the outbreak the leading chiefs at once became disunited; all were too selfishly interested in securing as much as they could for themselves in the general scramble, hardly corresponding with each other, even to the extent of furnishing that all-important item, good intelligence. In examining the rebel records and papers, I was much struck with the glaringly false news often intentionally communicated by the rebel authorities in one locality to those in another; still the sepoys had generally first-rate information, which was never conveyed in the form of correspondence. This information, if important, was always communicated orally by men who could be depended upon; an introduction in the fewest possible words being the only document with which they were entrusted, and this answered the purposes of a passport, besides guaranteeing that all the information they delivered might be received as incontrovertible.

For example, on one occasion in 1857, when I had been wandering alone on long marches day after day, without intermission, in company with the 15th Irregulars, whose intentions it was impossible not to distrust, I received information that Lucknow had been relieved, and the enemy driven out of the place Knowing that the 15th were interested, as the majority of their regiment were present at Lucknow, fighting against us, and thinking, moreover, that it might influence their own conduct, I gave the native officer the news; but he quietly answered, and with evident sincerity, "No, sir, that is not the case; the place has not been relieved." So often had I been deceived by our cruelly bad semi-official intelligence that I could not but think he might be right, or might even be aware of some unfavourable news; so, as a number of the men were standing round, I kept quiet, and the native officer's information turned out correct. At the time, it was a mystery to me how the intelligence could reach this native, when moving about day after day, without the possibility of any one knowing where he could be found, and the only solution of the difficulty would be that my party had fallen across one of the accredited intelligencers, whom the persevering activity of the rebel sepoys constantly scattered over the country, with the view of inducing those who had not yet mutinied to join their standard.

As the religious features of the revolt have been referred to, I may here add that, when conversing with Rajpoots and Chutries (the two classes of Hindoos most averse to our rule, because they were at one time supreme in the land), I often have been struck with observations conveying their impression that, with the suppression of the revolt, their religion,* not their race, had been conquered; and a deep-rooted conviction of this nature was implanted amongst a very large portion of the more ignorant Hindoo population in the North-West Provinces. But the Hindustani mind, as pliable as their bodies, seeing, for the time, that it is actually conquered, at once adapts itself to the supposed change, and gives in with a good grace. It even does more, for never amongst the descendants of the moon† has the success of Christian missionaries been so great in the Ganges-Jumna Doab, as since our reoccupation of that part of the country.

Both the Mahomedans and, in many respects, their

* The Seikhs, when ridiculing the sepoys, invariably termed them "Mâtâ deens," or foreheads of religion.

† The Rajpoots of the North-West Provinces are almost all Chundurbunsees, or descendants of the moon; those of Central India being Surujbunsees, or descendants of the sun. The former appear to be the finest race.

short-sighted dupes, the Hindoos, gloried in the revolt as the grand chance for a return to the unadulterated purity of their several religions. The Mahomedans, who generally, and to all appearance naturally, assumed the position of rulers during the revolt, took the most politic precautions to foster amongst the Hindoos this joyous feeling; that the sun, in fact, was going back on the dial, by constantly introducing strange contrasts with our previous rule. Thus, the killing of cattle was periodically interdicted by the Mahomedan authorities throughout the rebel tracts, and this, too, without a murmur from their co-religionists, who all, even the lowest rabble, thoroughly understood the game of their masters. Again, two Brahmuns were hanged at Furruckabad for committing adultery. Though the culprits were Brahmuns, the whole Hindoo population turned out to witness the execution, and applauded this delightful transition from English rule, at a time when they were trembling for their very existence, with a reign of terror supreme around them. On another occasion, English refined sugar, probably plundered from Cawnpore or Shahjehanpore, was offered for sale in the bazaar of Kumalgunj, when the Mahomedan authorities at once prosecuted with rigour this insult to Hindoo prejudices, the offending parties being fortunate in escaping with their lives.

But instances of this nature were innumerable, and every device that could possibly encourage or increase this religious fascination was at once adopted by both Hindoo and Mahomedan leaders, for they well knew that all would be lost if the transient impulses of their race could not be kept up to the mark. Apart from the antipathy of race, which must always receive its due share among the other incentives, the revolt of 1857 has, in reality, been nothing less than the last great stand made by the unrelenting hate of the false religions of India against Christian civilization, and, in the light of subsequent history, will be viewed as prompted more by that keen instinct engrafted in ignorance which so often transcends the calculations of reason, than as the result of a well-matured plan; and yet this outbreak was not totally deficient in design, which, through the peculiarities inherent in the race, but clumsily adapted itself to the spirit of the times.

APPENDIX.

APPENDIX.

[*Chapter* iv. *page* 77.]

The following narrative of the mutiny of the 5th Native Infantry at Saharunpore appeared in the *Lahore Chronicle* of the 29th of May, 1858, and could only have been written by the civil surgeon, who continued in Saharunpore throughout the disturbances of 1857 :—

"The 2nd of June was our critical day. When we now look back to it, we marvel how any of us escaped death. God's good providence shielded us, as, in a similar manner, it did many hundreds of our countrymen at that time of common peril.

"We had so often apprehended danger, that at last we fancied we were to enjoy an immunity from its evils. On that day, one or two of our party had been forewarned ; and although they communicated to us the information they got, yet we would not permit ourselves to believe that aught extraordinary would occur. We spent the day in our wonted manner, and, in the evening, formed our parties for the usual drive.

"The discontent and ill-suppressed disaffection of the sepoys of the 5th Native Infantry had reached such a pitch, that their commanding officer took the advice of the magistrate, and others in the station, as to the best line of policy to pursue with them. It was eventually agreed, that on that day the men should publicly be told, that if any, or all of their number, felt dissatisfied with the service, they were at liberty to take their discharge, receiving a certificate of the same, and every fraction of pay due to them.

"Accordingly, in the afternoon, the officer in command, with the magistrate and others, went down to the men. Contrary to our expectation, the proposal, when made, created the most violent opposition.

"Every imaginable argument was employed to convince the men that our plan ought to give them satisfaction; but it was soon very evident, that the mode we thought so natural and simple of settling the differences between us, was the very opposite to their wish. Whilst this unfruitful debate was proceeding, a very few of our party had gathered in front of the house, and were eagerly listening to an animated and graphic account of the battles on the Hindun, written by the late Commissioner of the Meeruth division, and were congratulating each other on the successful bravery of a handful of Europeans fighting under a fierce sun, when we were startled into action by the rapid discharge of musketry from the encampment of the 5th Native Infantry. We now felt that our hour of peril had come, but we did not shrink from it. Seizing our arms, we stood ready to meet the danger, our thoughts and anxieties, in the meantime, being with those of our number who were amongst the sepoys. At the first discharge, we thought all must have been shot; but great was our relief on looking towards the encampment to see three of the number running towards us.

"We now learned from a few hurried words, that, on the disaffected sepoys being urged to take their discharge, they seized their arms, and cried out, 'We do not want our discharge—we want to fight.' At this conjuncture, the officer who commanded the cavalry made an attempt to get to his men to call them out; but he was fired at so frequently, that he failed to effect his purpose, and so joined us at the house. At the same time, the magistrate, with a similar object, ran to call out a detachment of the 29th that was in charge of the stud treasure; but the men refused assistance, giving, as an excuse, that they could not leave the treasure.

"We now loaded our uncouth cannon, and got it into position. If we had misgivings as to its capacity of being safely discharged, we did not indulge them, deeming it wiser to run the risk of an explosion than to miss the opportunity of sending a heavy charge of canister amongst the foe. We waited in momentary expectation of an attack, thinking it most strange that we were left so long unmolested. It was not till much later in the evening that we learned that the mutiny was not general. A party stood by their officers, and gallantly defended them. The pay havildar, indeed, shot the ringleader almost at the very first outbreak. We saw this man lying cold and lifeless in the moonlight, the dark blood congealed on the mortal wound. A number of his comrades had gathered round him, and it was not difficult to guess their thoughts, from the excited and angry looks they wore. Indeed, it is a marvel what feeling restrained them on that evening from joining those who had openly mutinied; for it was not very many days later, that these very men, having first attempted the murder of their officers, deserted to Delhi.

"It was late when we sat down to dinner, and yet three of our party were still absent. The anxiety we felt on their account was soon removed by their appearance. They had a story of hair-breadth escapes to narrate. On returning from the evening drive, the horse they drove stumbled and fell. They were forced, therefore, to walk. On nearing the house, they heard the noise of firing, and the sepoy shouts of 'Mâr, mâr!' Not knowing what had happened, and being unarmed, they thought it best to make for the cavalry encampment. Walking towards it, a party of armed sepoys was seen approaching with rapid steps, who, when they observed three unarmed Europeans, renewed their fiendish cry of 'Mâr, mâr!'

and ran to intercept them. In this they well nigh succeeded. It was only by extreme fleetness of foot, called forth by the imminency of danger, that our friends escaped the murderous clutches of their enemy, and only by excessive wariness that they avoided being shot, for they were fired upon frequently, and from short insignificant distances.

"This took place in full view of the troopers of the 4th Lancers, but they did not take one step to shield their officers from danger; however, they professed the greatest pleasure at the escape."

[*Chapter* vii. *page* 125.]

The following is extracted from Lieutenant Boisragon's report to his commanding officer, of the expedition to Nookur, Khoondah, &c.; and in reply to which our party received the thanks of General Bernard, then commanding at Delhi.

"About 6 A.M. on the 22nd, we reached the camp, where our arrival was heartily welcomed. I had just ordered my men to fall out, warning them to be ready at a moment's notice, when we heard the dhôls and shouts of a large body close to our camp. I was sure that the arrival of my detachment was unknown to the insurgents, and, therefore, directed the men by word of mouth; told off a party of thirty under the sergeant-major to advance skirmishing; sent a party of twelve, under Mr. Wilcocks, into a heavy tope of trees to protect our flank on that side, and detached the cavalry, consisting of about forty sowars, under Mr. Robertson, to the open ground on the right; while I brought up the rest of my men through a very heavy mango tope. With the assistance of the cover from the trees and deep ditch, the whole party sneaked up to the skirmishers, and in concealment. During this time the insurgents, having only seen about thirty men, advanced in a body. Unfortunately, however, before we had all got properly into position, the order was given, they say by the sergeant-major, to commence firing, the enemy having been peppering at us the whole time. As they were still about 180 yards off, and not wishing to warn the enemy by bugle sounds, I went out in front to stop the firing on our side. While trying to do this, their shots fell close to me; on seeing which the men rushed out of the ditch and fired, and, with a cheer, went on, despising numbers or distance,—quite forgetting that with forty rounds of ammunition, and an eighteen miles' march, they had no chance in running with the enemy. While this was going on in my front, Mr. Robertson was attacked by a large body on the right, and had some narrow escapes from their bullets; one man (an amateur city sowar) being killed close to him. As soon as the party in our front gave way, the whole 600 or 700 took to their heels. We pursued for about five miles, overtaking numbers, and finding many concealed in trees. The loss on the enemy's side must have been fifty or sixty, while we escaped without a scratch, with the exception of the city man alluded to. We took several prisoners, from whom we obtained much information, and also the names of the lumbardars, one of whom was among the killed.

"The next morning, June 24th, we started at 2 A.M., and marched along quietly until near Naygoan, one of the villages that we attacked the first day, and where we were informed a large body were waiting in ambush for us. All night we moved along cautiously, a reconnoitring party going on under Mr. Robertson, while I brought my men right under the walls on all three sides. After some little delay, owing to the intense darkness rendering everything invisible, we got through the village, empty, as usual, but showing symptoms of very late occupation. With day came rain, but the men were all anxious to push on to meet Futtuah, for whose apprehension, with Mr. Robertson's sanction, I offered 200 rupees. During our arrangements of observation at Naygoan, Mr. Robertson had gone on a mile or so in advance, with thirty of my men and some sowars, and we did not overtake them until we got to Mohunpore, where their further progress was disputed by an obstruction in the shape of a few bullets fired at Mr. Robertson, who, seeing a large collection of men, demanded of the lumbardars to account for the gathering. They, however, sent word back that, if the sahib wanted them, he might go into the village and fetch them himself. On my arrival, we made arrangements to attack the village, out of which we drove them in a very few minutes, pursued them a short distance, and killed six, one of whom was recognized as an escaped prisoner from the Meeruth gaol, and who, only two days previously, had murdered a bunyah at Gungoh. We took several prisoners, who corroborated the statements of those taken at Nookur, that Bhooda Kheree was the leading village in the rebellion.

"We now went straight to Bhooda Kheree, where we were informed there were two small guns mounted on the towers of an old Mahratta fort in the village. This was my first point of attack, and the parties were told off for either of these towers; but the place had been abandoned, so with the elephants I demolished 'the would-be king's' place. We then marched into Gungoh, another seven miles, which we reached about 2 P.M., having marched fully twenty-one miles.

"On the morning of the 26th, we started at 1.30 A.M. to attack Khoondah. As it was a good road, I took the Goorkhas down in the hackeries, which I intended making use of as barricades, should necessity compel me. During the 25th we had most unpleasant reports regarding the irregulars. I will, however, give the irregulars the credit to say they had hitherto done their work thoroughly, though they were very troublesome in camp about supplies. However, I kept them between the Seikhs (than whose conduct throughout nothing could have been more satisfactory) and the Goorkhas. When nearing the place where we expected to find the insurgents, I dismounted my sepoys from the hackeries, and despatched reconnoitring parties under Messrs. Robertson, Colledge, and Wilcocks. Mr. Robertson's party had not left me five minutes when we heard some six or eight shots, and Mr. Robertson galloped in to say that a party were in front, and that he had been fired at by a number of men amongst the trees. We all got together and advanced as quickly as we could. About 150 yards on we came in sight of the villages Oomerpore (to our left), Shahpore (on raised ground in the centre), and Manpore (on our right). All round and close to Oomerpore was an extensive tope of mango trees, with underwood and plantain groves. From Oomerpore to Manpore must be about half a mile, and the whole of this extent was covered with human beings, in some places ten or twenty deep. We saw a goodly party of horsemen, and the whole force could not have numbered under 3,000 men. The extent of ground covered by the insurgents prevented my attacking them in lines, so I divided the whole force into two divisions, flanking each with cavalry, and a party of cavalry in the centre. Mr. Hyde took the cavalry on the left flank, and I detached the sergeant-major and Mr. Wilcocks to assist Mr. Robertson with the left division; Mr. Colledge accompanied me with the right. The two divisions attacked them on either flank, beating them up towards Shahpore. This was very soon done, and they all amassed between Shahpore and Oomerpore, where they kept firing at us, until the party under Mr. Robertson gave them a volley, followed by successful shots from our side. As soon as we saw the enemy wavering (we had all met by this time), we gave a cheer and charged, when they scattered. We found a good many had been killed by the volley, and, as we wanted to give them a good lesson, I allowed my men to follow as they liked. Mr. Robertson had galloped off with the cavalry in pursuit, and gave a first-rate account of them. We chased them for some two miles, when, coming on an extensive thick jungle, I sounded the assembly; and, from the accounts of the officers with the various parties, we calculated their killed to be upwards of 150. The main body of the runaways having turned towards Khoondah Kulân, we marched on to it, coming across numbers of dead bodies and men concealed in wells and trees. On arriving before Khoondah, we saw a large body of men behind trees and walls, who immediately began firing on us. Mr. Robertson on one side, and Mr. Colledge on the other, went off with the cavalry to prevent their escape from the rear of the village; but this a large party effected, though numbers were driven back into the village and plantain gardens. It was here that a Seikh trooper was wounded by a bullet in the arm, and another's horse killed. Several men were concealed in their houses, and attacked our Goorkhas as they went through; but they paid dearly for their rashness, as our men spared none of them, and upwards of seventy were killed near and about the village."

THE END.

London: Printed by Smith, Elder & Co., Little Green Arbour Court, Old Bailey.